Agricultural Production Economics

THE ART OF PRODUCTION THEORY

DAVID L. DEBERTIN
University of Kentucky

This is a book of full-color illustrations intended for use as a companion to 428-page *Agricultural Production Economics, Second Edition*. Each of the 98 pages of illustrations is a large, full-color version of the corresponding numbered figure in the book *Agricultural Production Economics, Second Edition*. The illustrations are each a labor of love by the author representing a combination of science and art. They combine modern computer graphics technologies with the author's skills as both as a production economist and as a technical graphics artist.

Technologies used in making the illustrations trace the evolution of computer graphics over the past 30 years. Many of the hand-drawn illustrations were initially drawn using the *Draw Partner* routines from *Harvard Graphics*®. Wire-grid 3-D illustrations were created using *SAS Graph*®. Some illustrations combine hand-drawn lines using *Draw Partner* and the draw features of Microsoft *PowerPoint*® with computer-generated graphics from *SAS*®. As a companion text to *Agricultural Production Economics, Second Edition*, these color figures display the full vibrancy of the modern production theory of economics.

© 2012 David L. Debertin
Second Printing, December, 2012

David L. Debertin
University of Kentucky,
Department of Agricultural Economics
400 C.E.B. Bldg.
Lexington, KY 40546-0276

Debertin, David L.
        Agricultural Production Economics
        The Art of Production Theory

  1. Agricultural production economics
  2. Agriculture–Economic aspects–Econometric models

ISBN- 13: 978-1470129262
ISBN- 10: 1470129264

BISAC: Business and Economics/Economics/Microeconomics

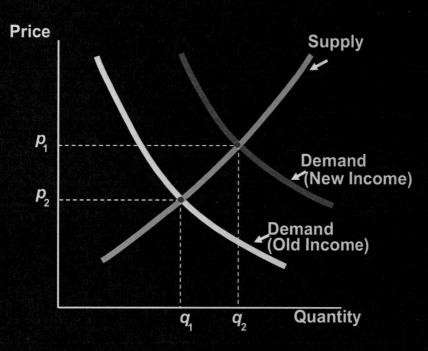

Figure 1.1 Supply and Demand

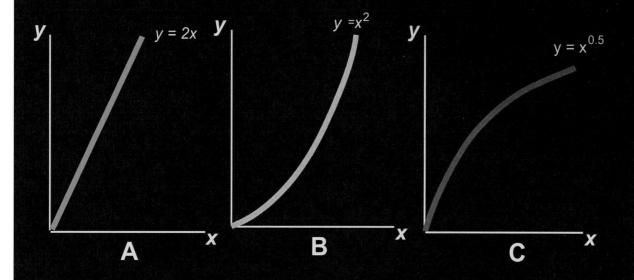

Figure 2.1 Three Production Functions

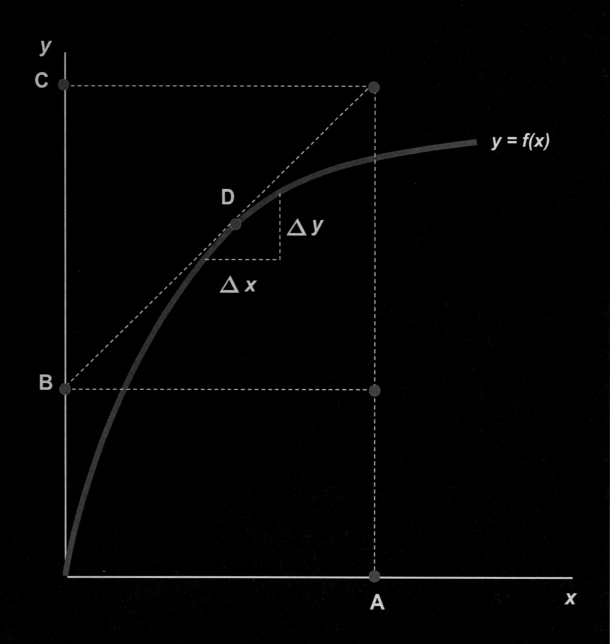

Figure 2.2 Approximate and Exact *MPP*

2

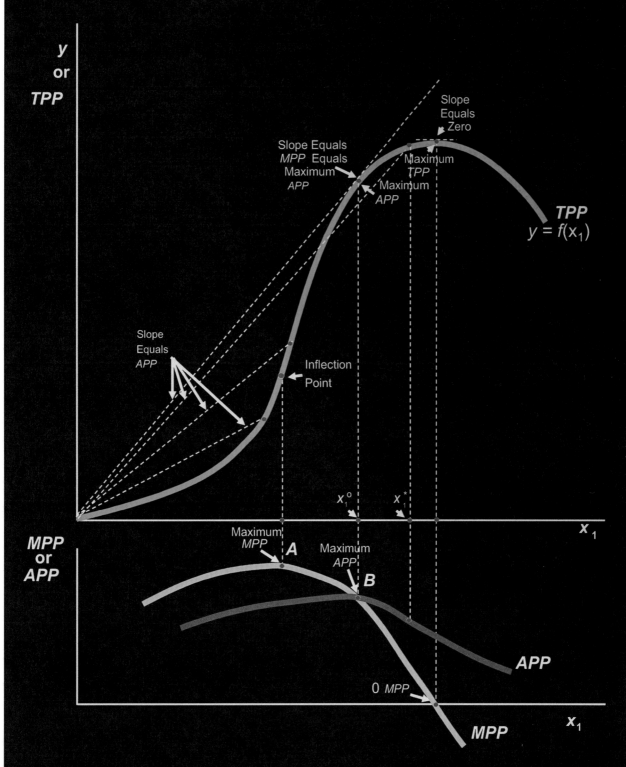

Figure 2.3 A Neoclassical Production Function

3

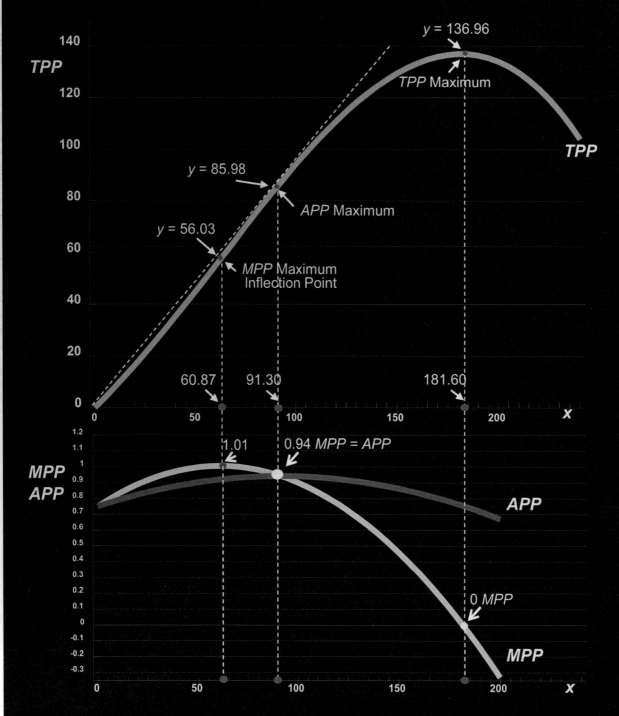

Figure 2.4 *TPP, MPP* and *APP* for Corn (*y*) Response to Nitrogen (*x*) Based on Table 2.5 Data

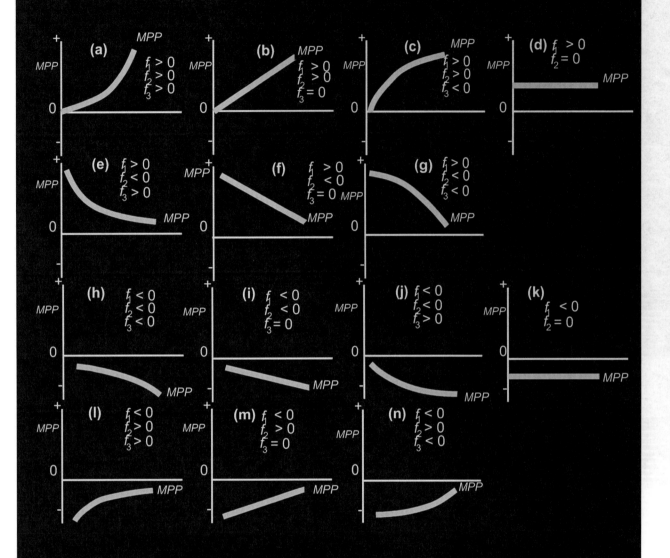

Figure 2.5 *MPP*'s for the Production Function $y = f(x)$

5

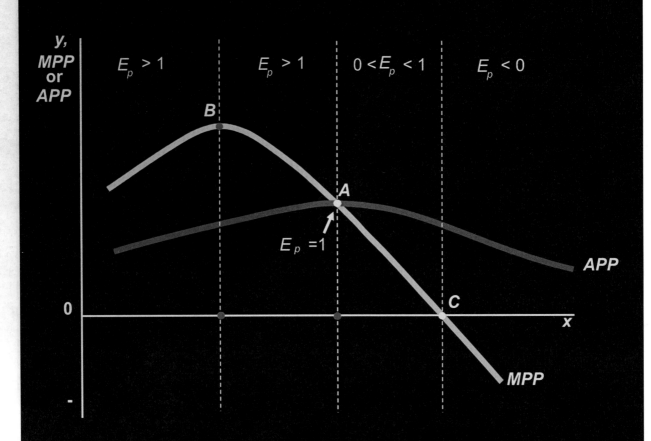

Figure 2.6 *MPP, APP* and the Elasticity of Production

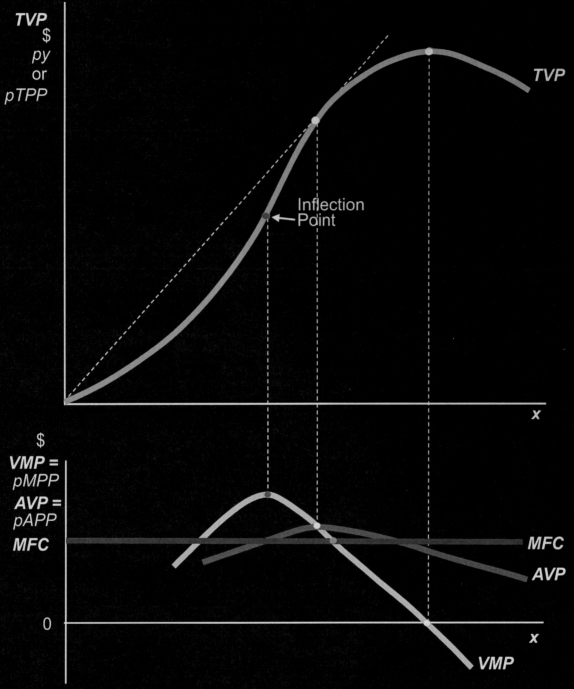

Figure 3.1 The Relationship Between *TVP*, *VMP*, *AVP*, and *MFC*

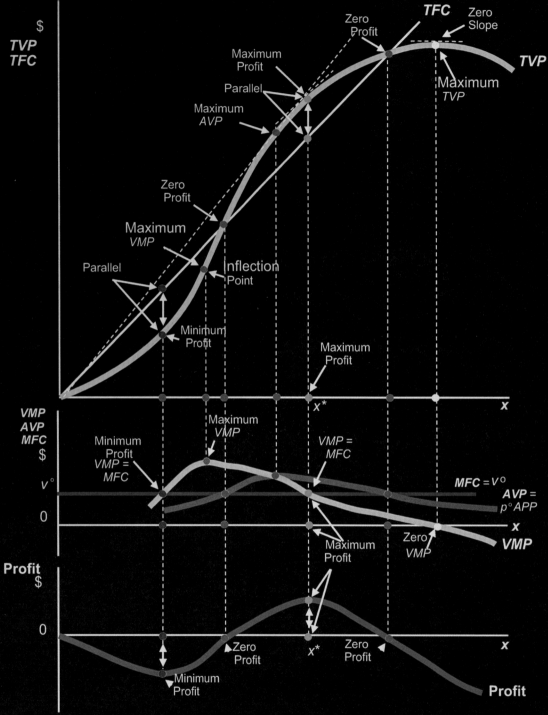

Figure 3.2 *TVP, TFC, VMP, MFC* and Profit

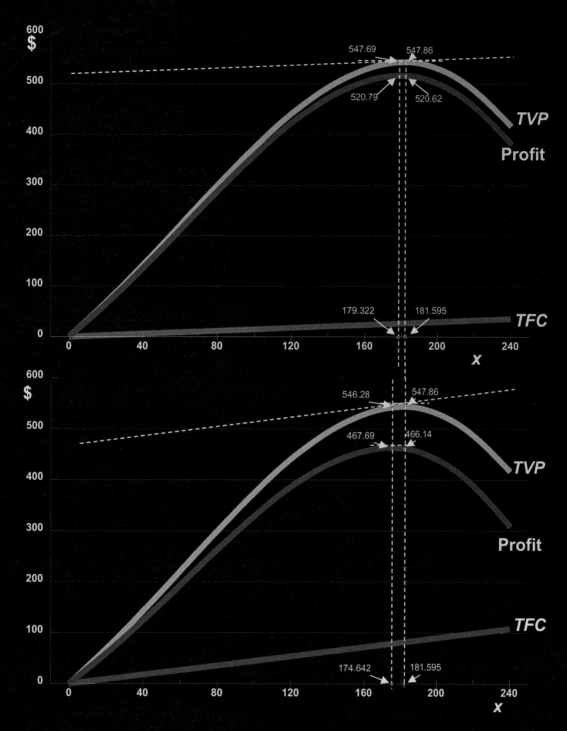

Figure 3.3 *TVP, TFC* and Profit (Top and Second Panel)

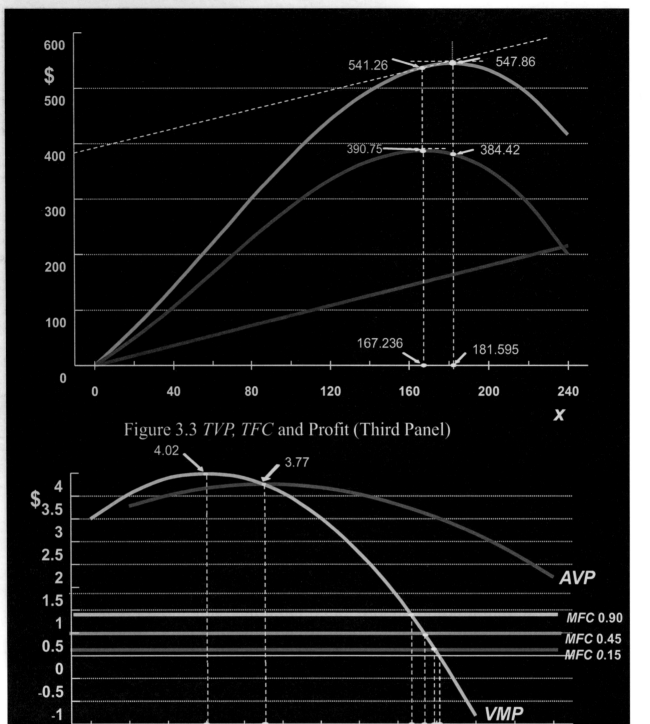

Figure 3.3 *TVP, TFC* and Profit (Third Panel)

Figure 3.3 Profit Maximization under Varying
Assumptions with Respect to Input Prices (Bottom Panel)

10

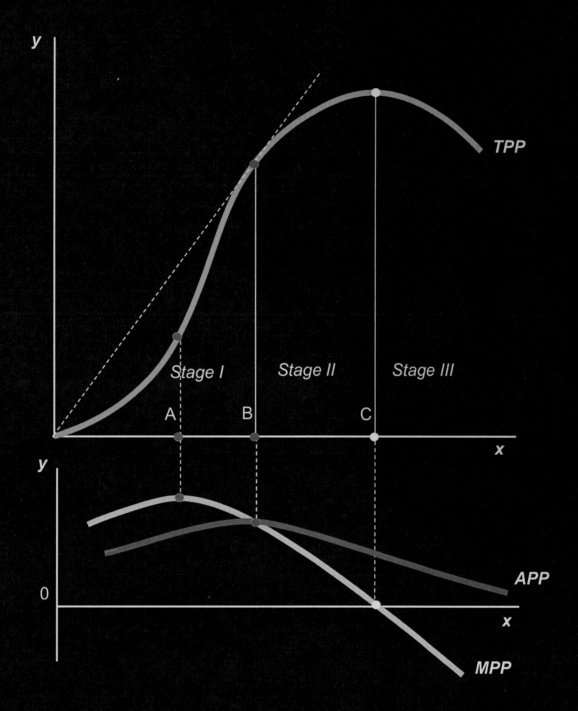

Figure 3.4 Stages of Production and the Neoclassical Production Function

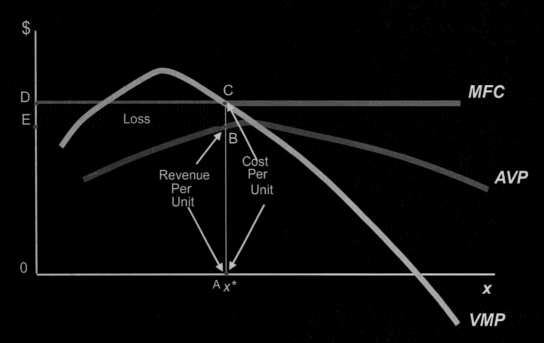

Figure 3.5 If *VMP* is Greater than *AVP*, the Farmer Will Not Operate

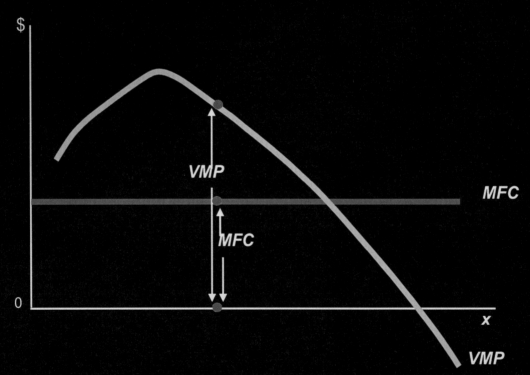

Figure 3.6   The Relationship Between *VMP* and *MFC* Illustrating the Imputed Value of an Input

12

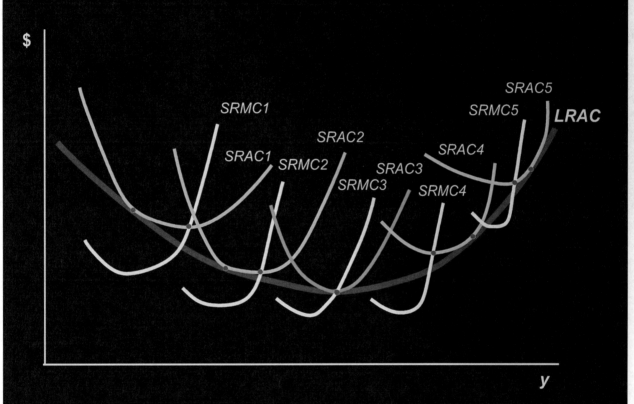

Figure 4.1 Short and Long Run Average and Marginal Cost
with Envelope Long Run Average Cost

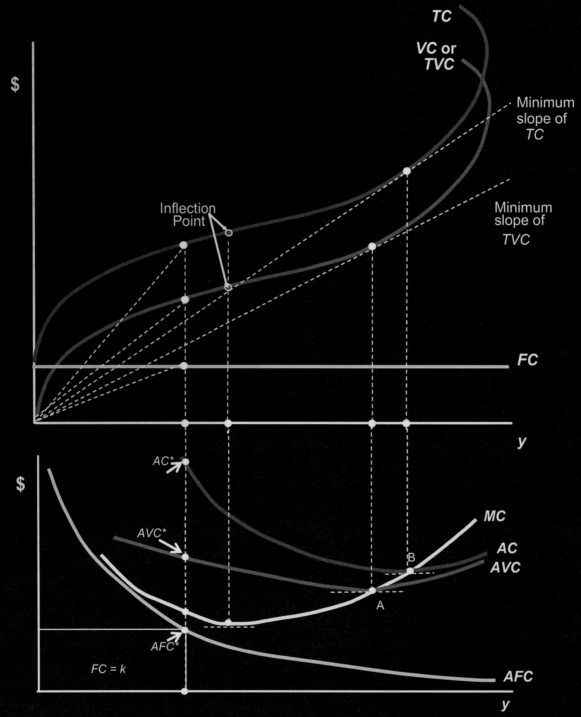

Figure 4.2 Cost Functions on the Output Side

14

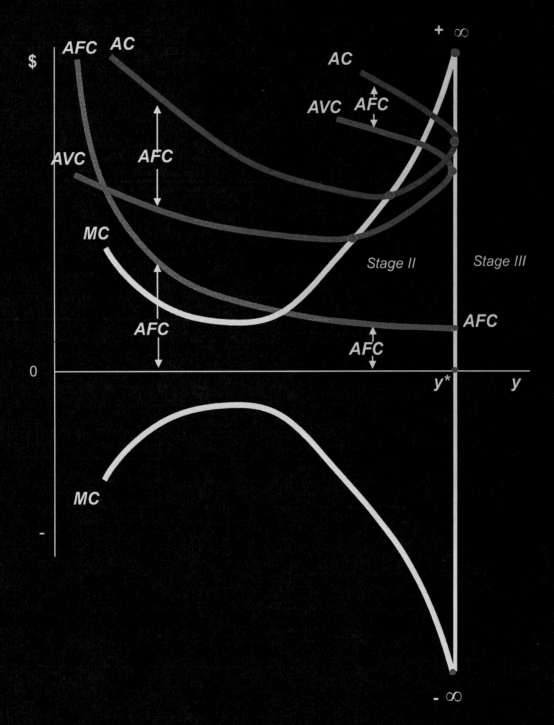

Figure 4.3 Behavior of Cost Curves as Output
Approaches a Technical Maximum y^*

15

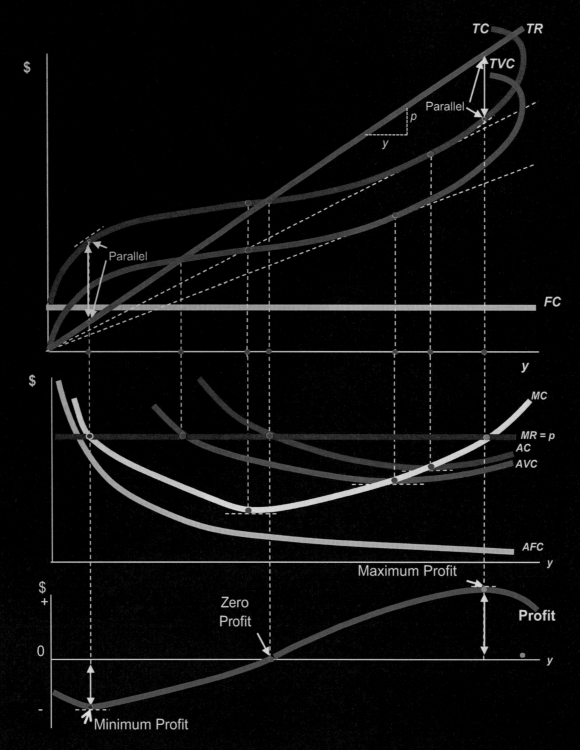

Figure 4.4 Cost Functions and Profit Functions

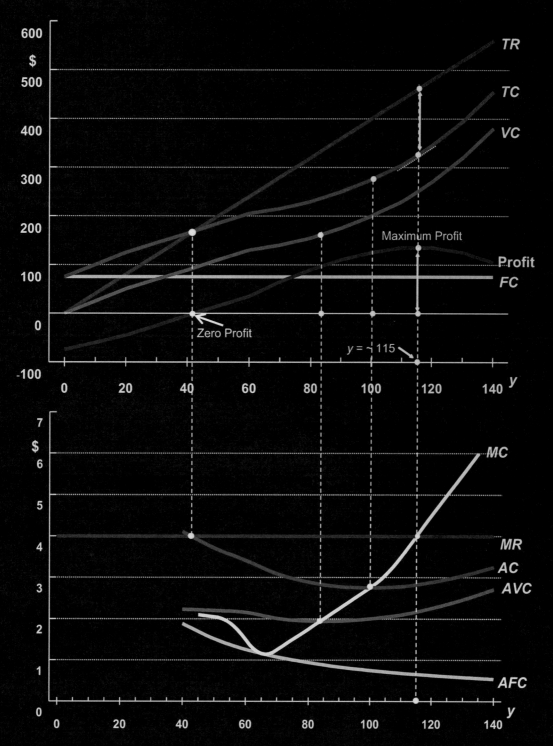

Figure 4.5 The Profit-Maximizing Output Level
Based on Data Contained in Table 4.1

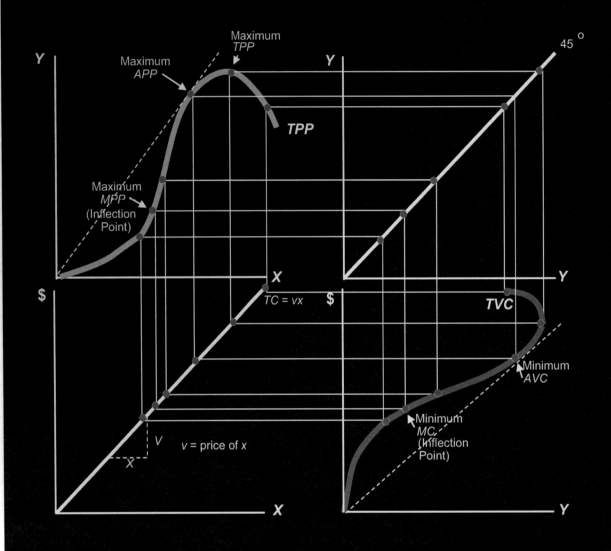

Figure 4.6 A Cost Function as an Inverse Production Function

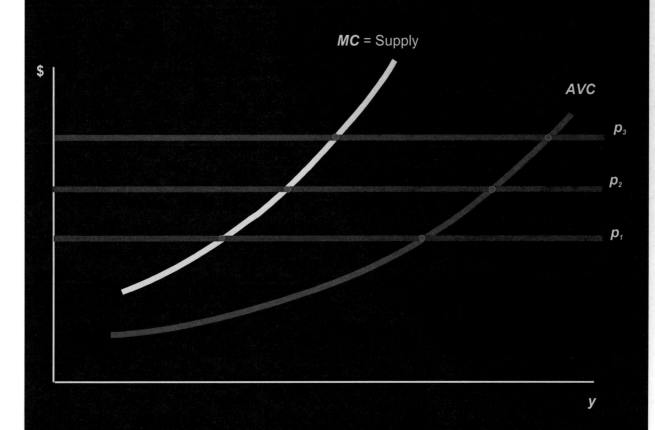

Figure 4.7 Aggregate Supply When the Ratio $MC/AC = 1/b$
and b is less than 1

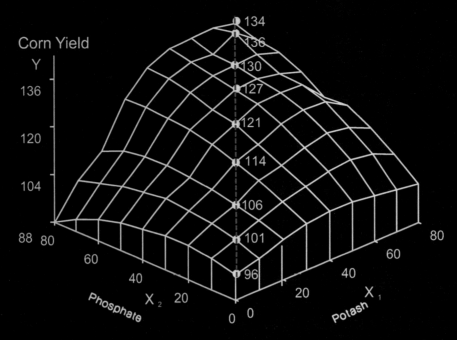

Figure 5.1 Production Response Surface Based
on Data Contained in Table 5.1

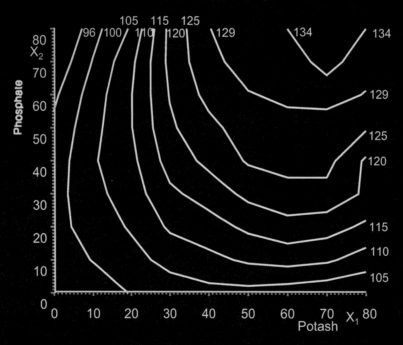

Figure 5.2 Isoquants for the Production Surface in
Figure 5.1 Based on Data Contained in Table 5.1

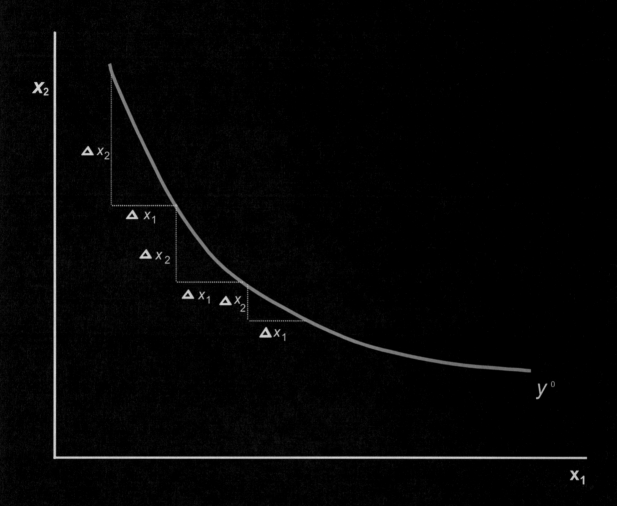

Figure 5.3 Illustration of Diminishing *MRS* x_1x_2

21

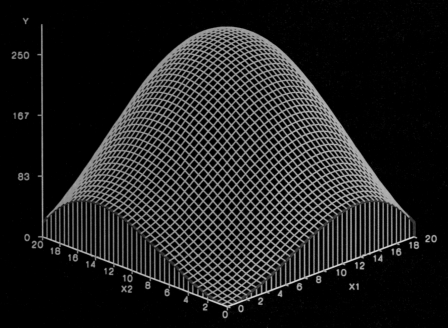

Figure 5.4 Isoquants and a Production Surface (Panel A)

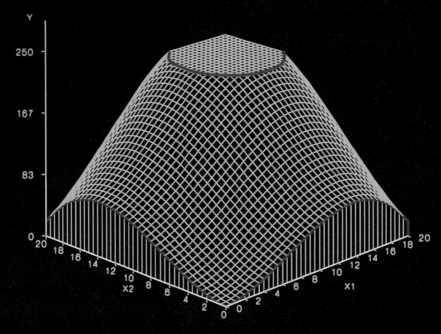

Figure 5.4 Isoquants and a Production Surface (Panel B)

22

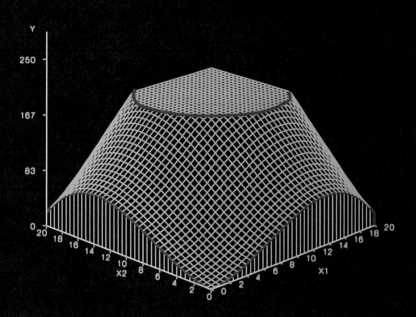

Figure 5.4 Isoquants and a Production Surface (Panel C)

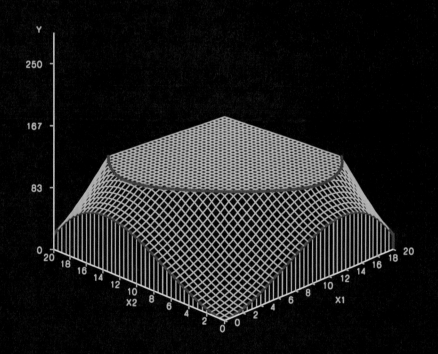

Figure 5.4 Isoquants and a Production Surface (Panel D)

23

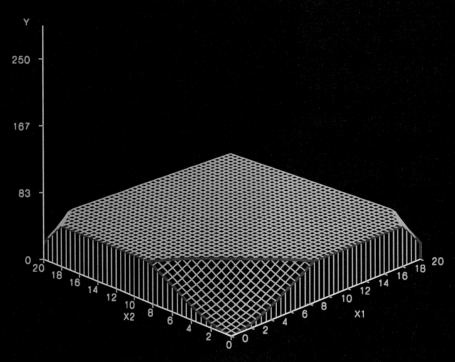

Figure 5.4 Isoquants and a Production Surface (Panel E)

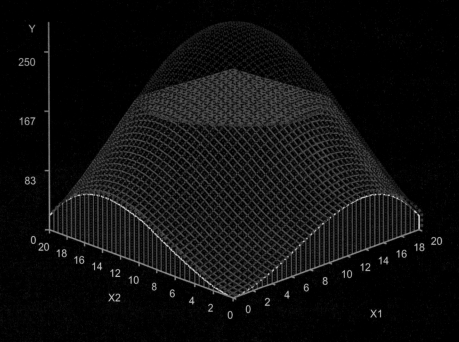

Figure 5.4 Isoquants and a Production Surface (Panel F)

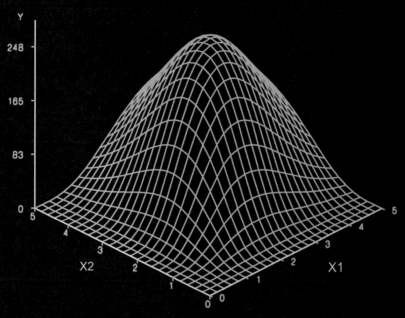

Figure 5.5 Some Possible Production
   Surfaces and Isoquant Map   A .The Production Surface

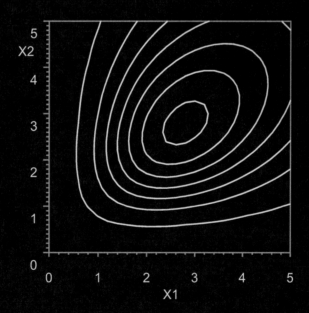

Figure 5.5 Some Possible Production
   Surfaces and Isoquant Map   B. The Isoquant Map

25

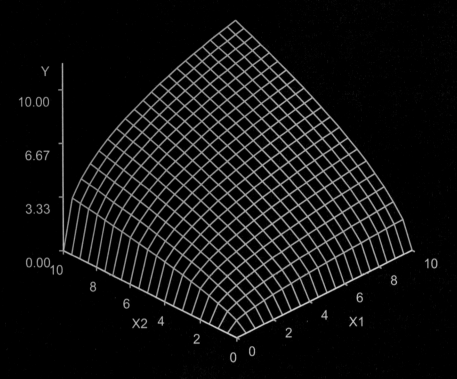

Figure 5.5 Some Possible Production
Surfaces and Isoquant Map   C . The Production Surface

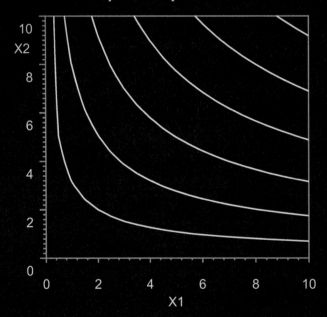

Figure 5.5 Some Possible Production
Surfaces and Isoquant Map   D . The Isoquants

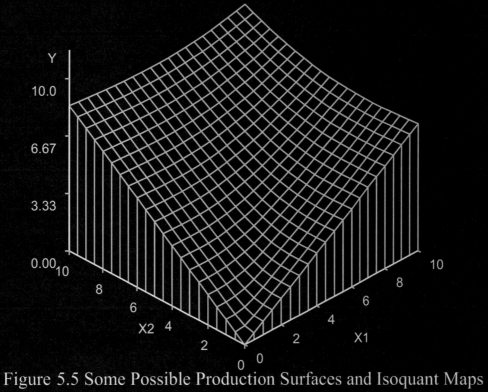

Figure 5.5 Some Possible Production Surfaces and Isoquant Maps
E. The Production Surface

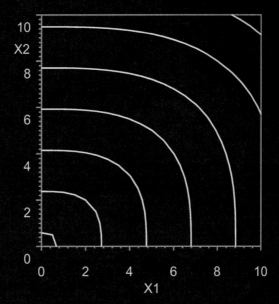

Figure 5.5 Some Possible Production Surfaces and Isoquant Maps
F. The Isoquants

27

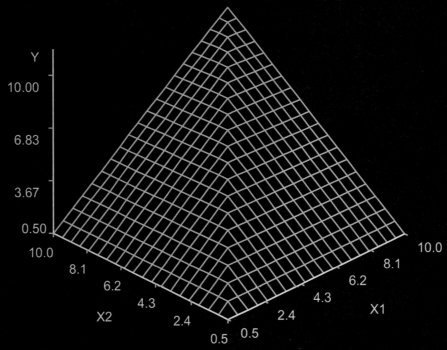

Figure 5.5 Some Possible Production Surfaces and Isoquant Maps
K. The Production Surface

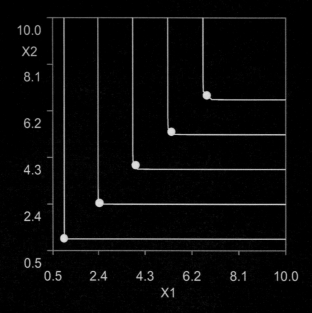

Figure 5.5 Some Possible Production Surfaces and Isoquant Maps
L. The Isoquants

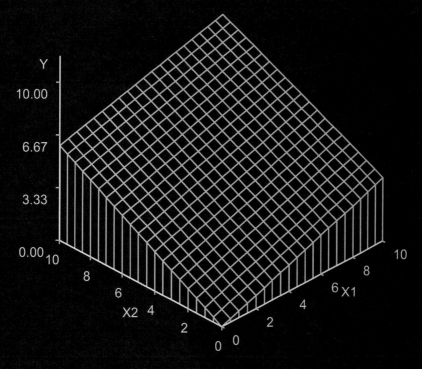

Figure 5.5 Some Possible Production Surfaces and Isoquant Maps
G.   The Production Surface

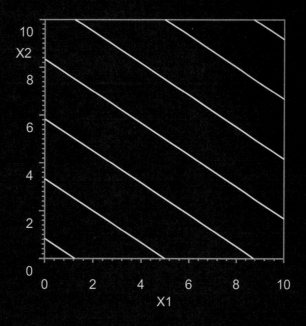

Figure 5.5 Some Possible Production Surfaces and Isoquant Maps
H. The Isoquants

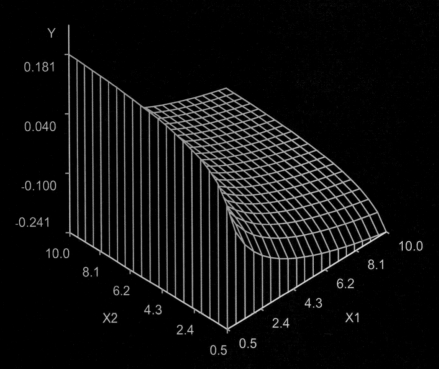

Figure 5.5 Some Possible Production Surfaces and Isoquant Maps
I. The Production Surface

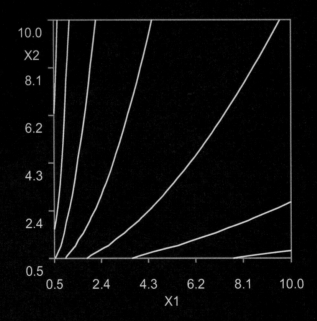

Figure 5.5 Some Possible Production Surfaces and Isoquant Maps
J. The Isoquants

30

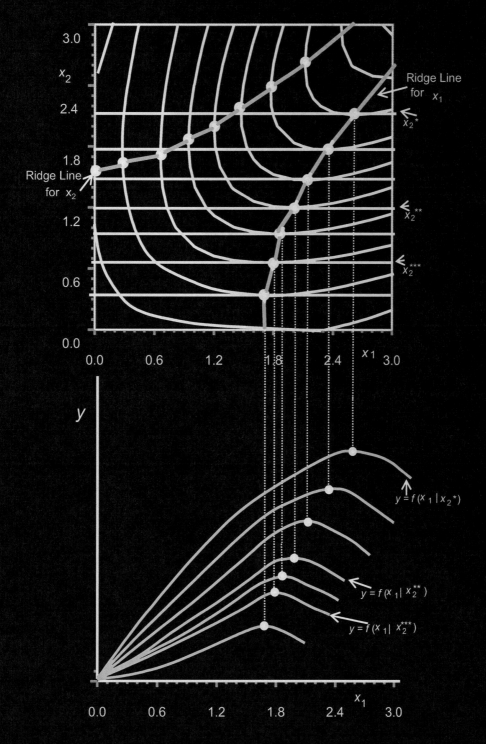

Figure 5.6 Ridge Lines and a Family of Production Functions
For Input x_1

31

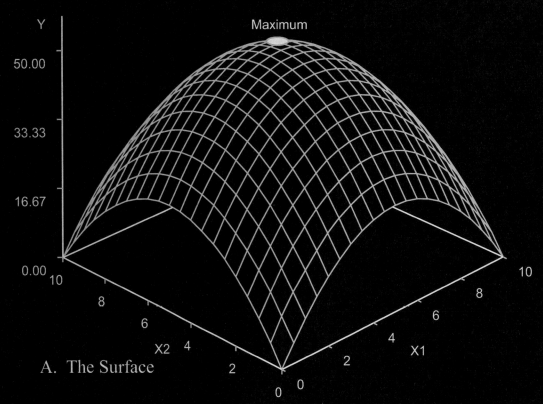

A. The Surface

Figure 6.1 Alternative Surfaces and Contours Illustrating
Second Order Conditions

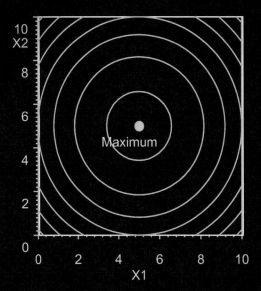

B. The Contour Lines

Figure 6.1 Alternative Surfaces and Contours Illustrating
Second Order Conditions

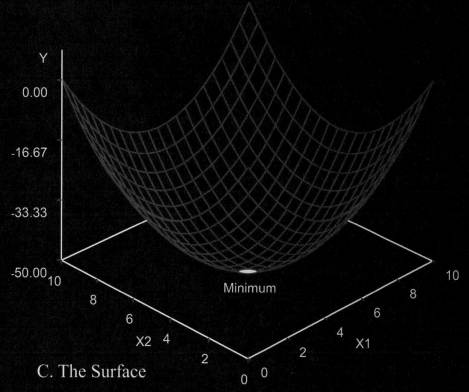

C. The Surface

Figure 6.1 Alternative Surfaces and Contours Illustrating
Second Order Conditions

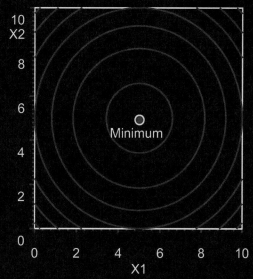

D. The Contour Lines

Figure 6.1 Alternative Surfaces and Contours Illustrating
Second Order Conditions

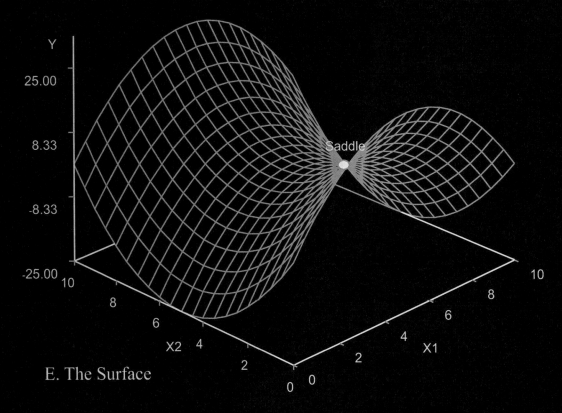

E. The Surface

Figure 6.1 Alternative Surfaces and Contours Illustrating
Second Order Conditions

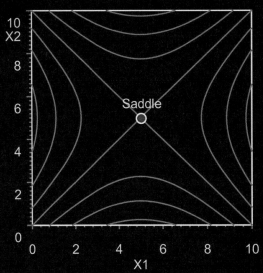

F. The Contour Lines

Figure 6.1 Alternative Surfaces and Contours Illustrating
Second Order Conditions

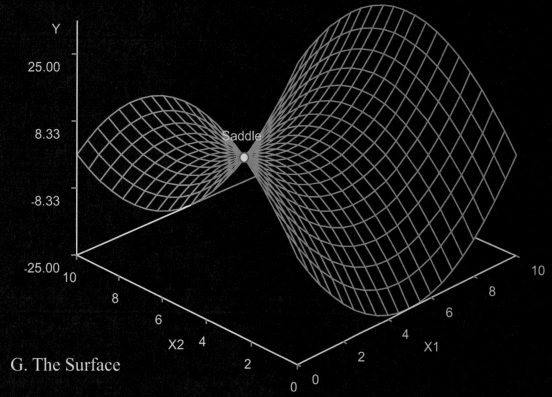

G. The Surface

Figure 6.1 Alternative Surfaces and Contours Illustrating
Second Order Conditions

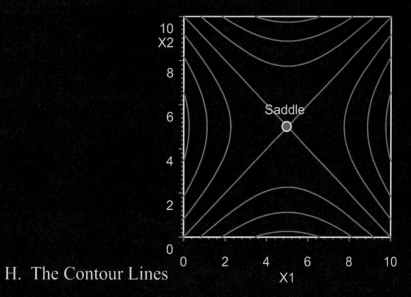

H. The Contour Lines

Figure 6.1 Alternative Surfaces and Contours Illustrating
Second Order Conditions

35

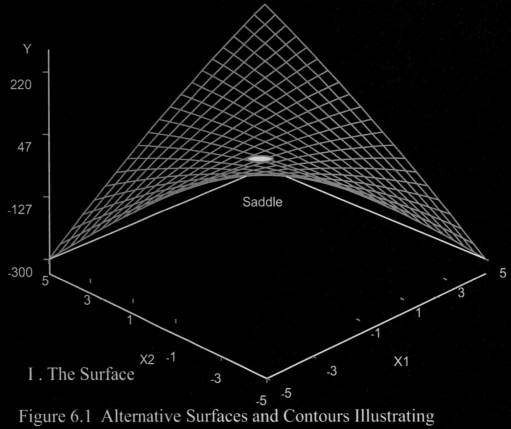

I . The Surface

Figure 6.1 Alternative Surfaces and Contours Illustrating
Second Order Conditions

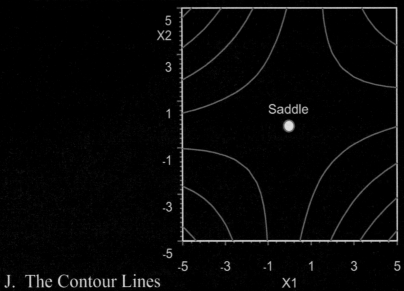

J. The Contour Lines

Figure 6.1   Alternative Surfaces and Contours Illustrating
Second Order Conditions

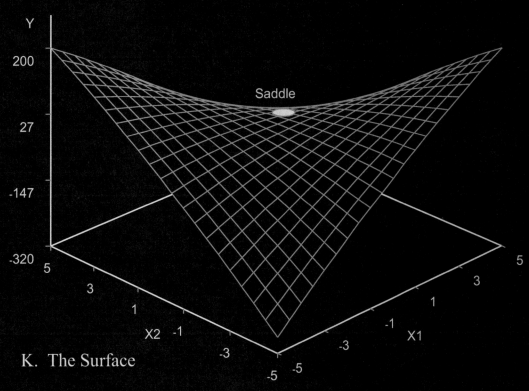

K. The Surface

Figure 6.1 Alternative Surfaces and Contours Illustrating
Second Order Conditions

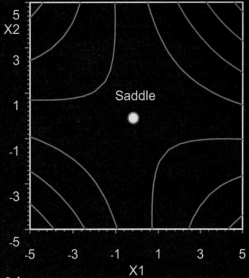

I. The Contour Lines

Figure 6.1 Alternative Surfaces and Contours Illustrating
Second Order Conditions

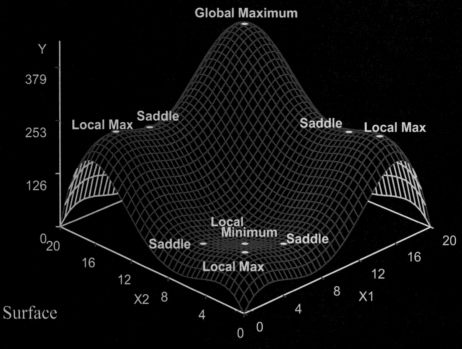

Surface

Figure 6.2 Critical Values for the Polynomial $y = 40\,x_1 - 12\,x_1^2$
$+ 1.2\,x_1^3 - 0.035x_1^4 + 40\,x_2 - 12\,x_2^2 + 1.2\,x_2^3 - 0.035x_2^4$

Contour Lines

Figure 6.2 Critical Values for the Polynomial $y = 40\,x_1 - 12\,x_1^2$
$+ 1.2\,x_1^3 - 0.035x_1^4 + 40\,x_2 - 12\,x_2^2 + 1.2\,x_2^3 - 0.035x_2^4$

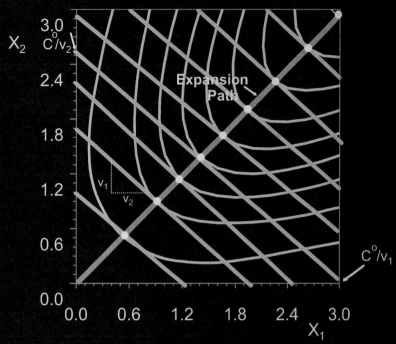

Figure 7.1 Iso-outlay Lines and the Isoquant Map

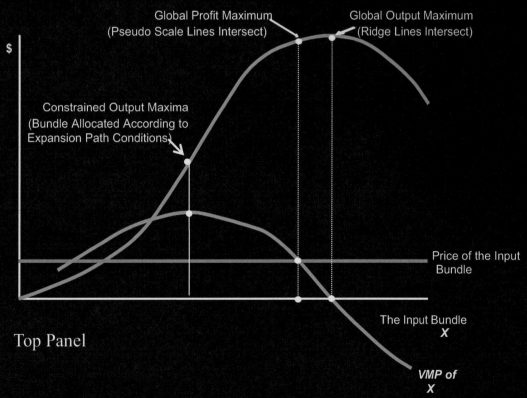

Top Panel

Figure 7.2 Global Output and Profit Maximization for the Bundle 39

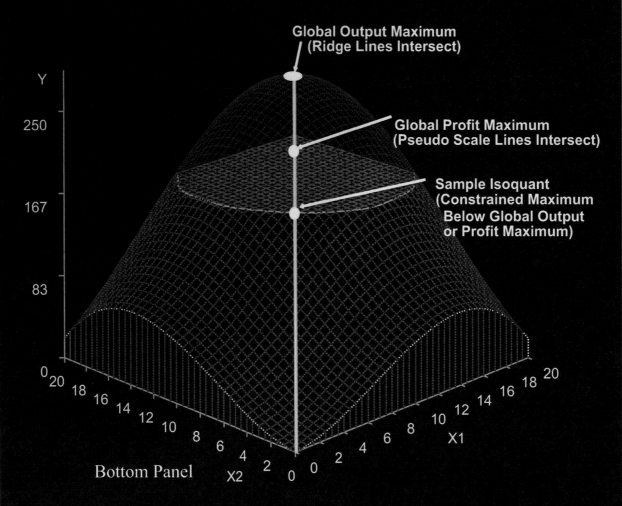

Figure 7.2 Global Output and Profit Maximization for the Bundle

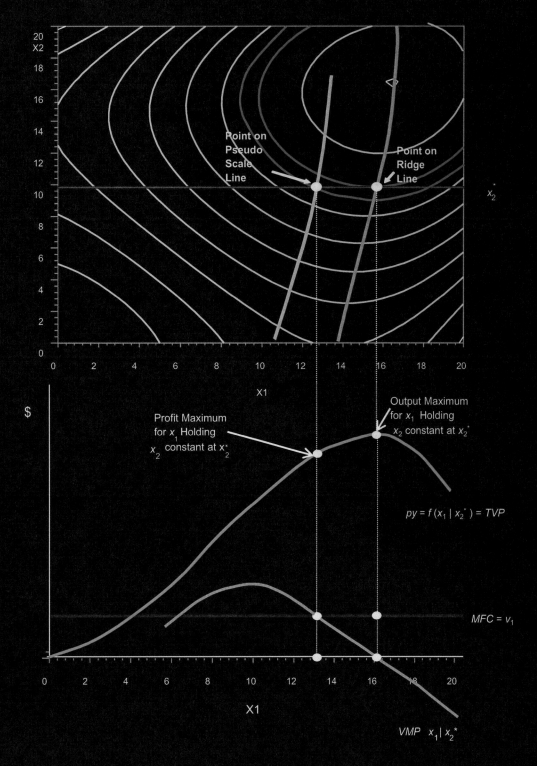

Figure 7.3 Deriving a Point on a Pseudo Scale Line

41

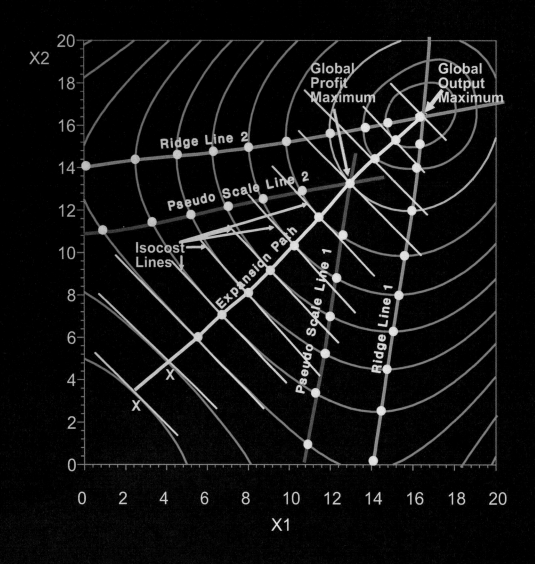

Figure 7.4 The Complete Factor-Factor Model

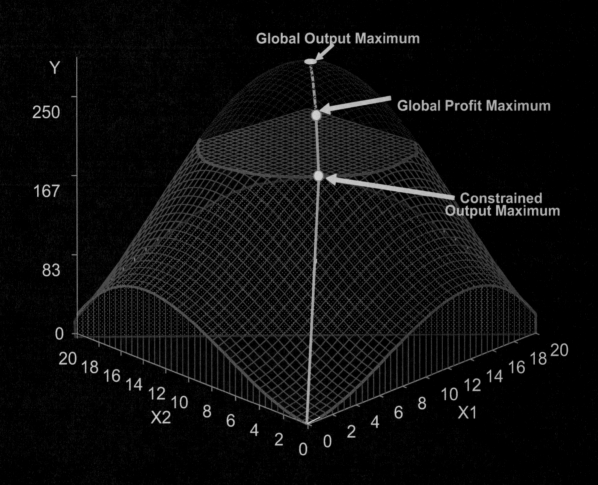

Figure 7.5 Constrained and Global Profit and Output Maxima
along the Expansion Path

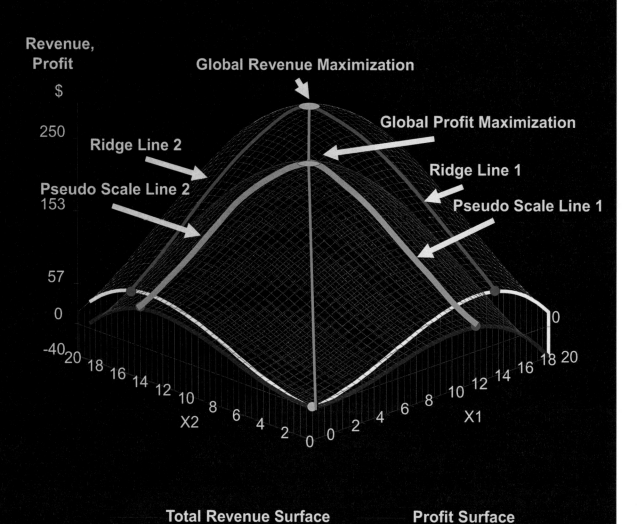

Figure 8.1 *TVP*- and Profit-Maximizing Surfaces

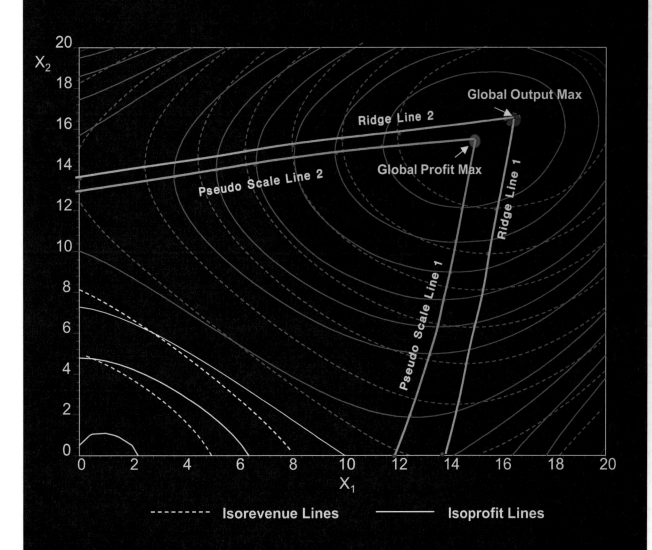

Figure 8.2 Isorevenue and Isoproduct Contours

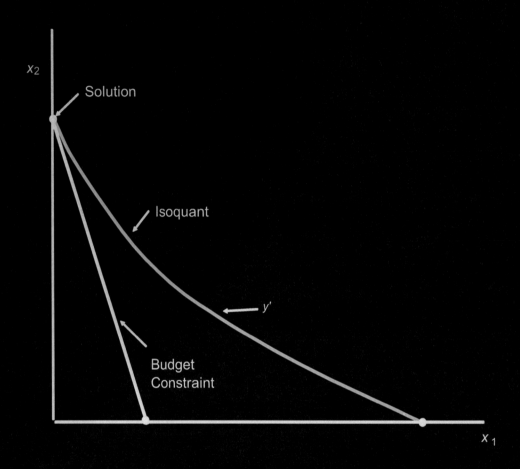

Figure 8.3 A Corner Solution

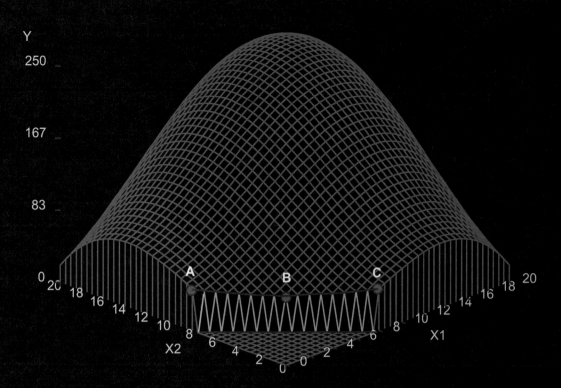

Figure 8.4 A.   Point B Less than A and C

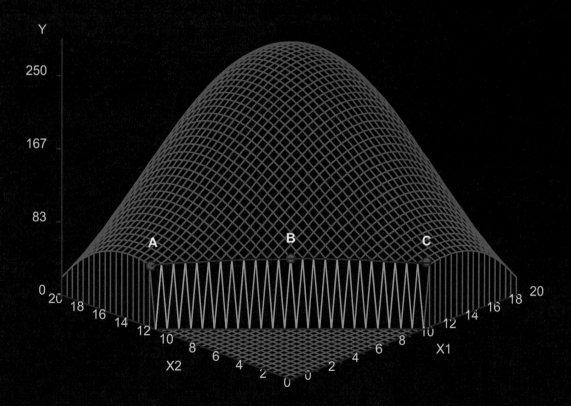

Figure 8.4 B.   Point B Equal to A and C

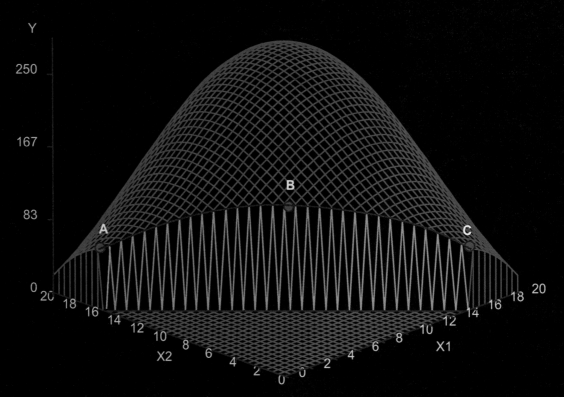

Figure 8.4 C .   Point B Greater than A and C

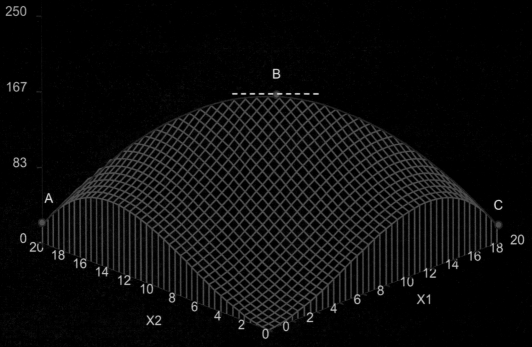

Figure 8.4 D.   Point B Greater than A and C

48

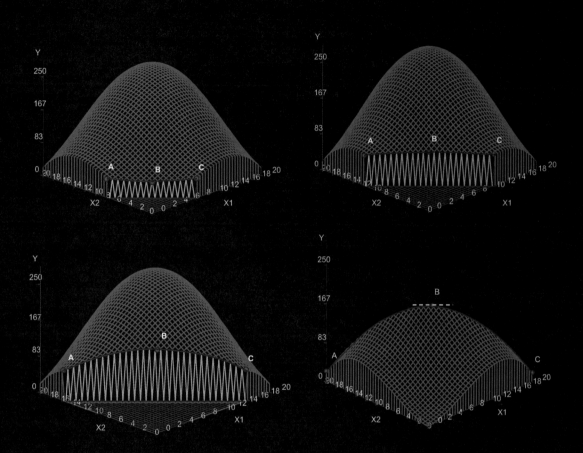

Figure 8.4 Constrained Maximization under Alternative
Isoquant Convexity or Concavity Conditions

49

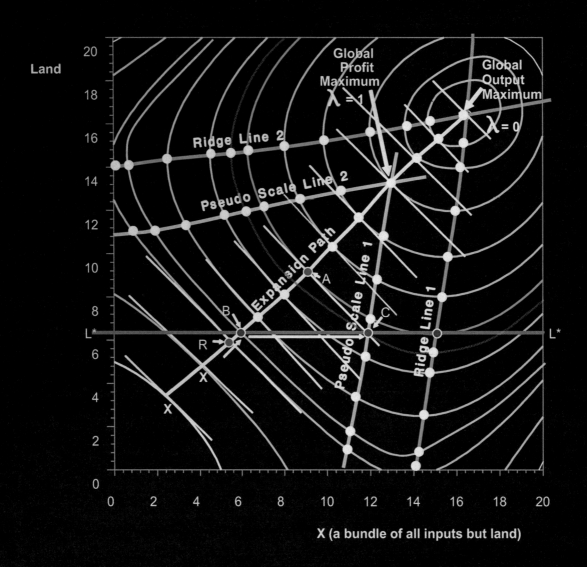

Figure 8.5 The Acreage Allotment Problem

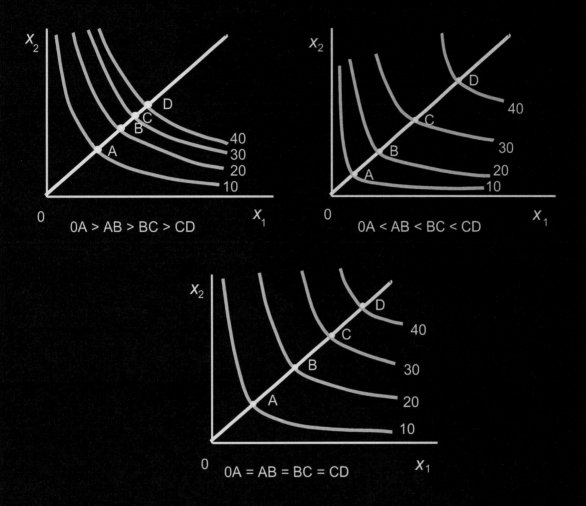

Figure 9.1 Economies, Diseconomies and Constant Returns to Scale
For a Production Function with Two Inputs

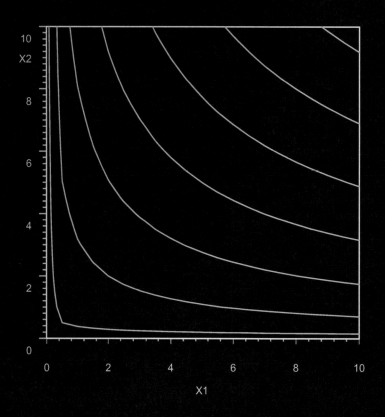

Figure 10.1 Isoquants for the Cobb-Douglas Production Function

52

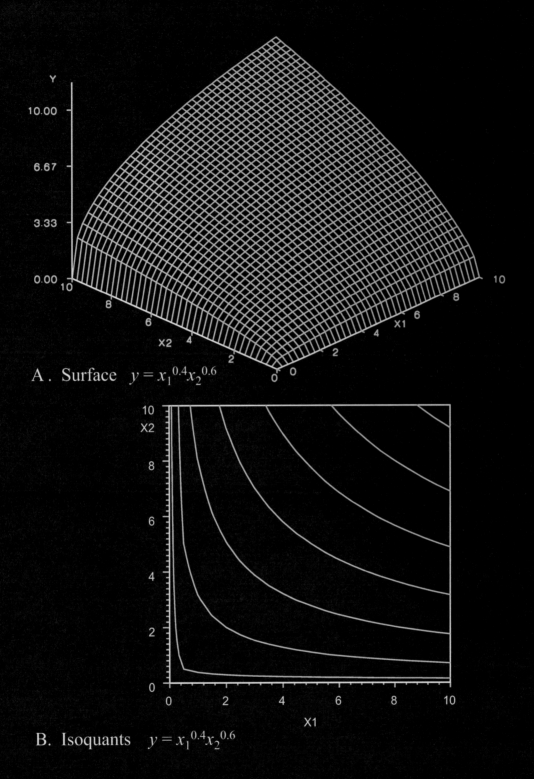

A . Surface $y = x_1^{0.4} x_2^{0.6}$

B. Isoquants $y = x_1^{0.4} x_2^{0.6}$

Figure 10.2 Surfaces and Isoquants for the Cobb-Douglas
Type Production Function

53

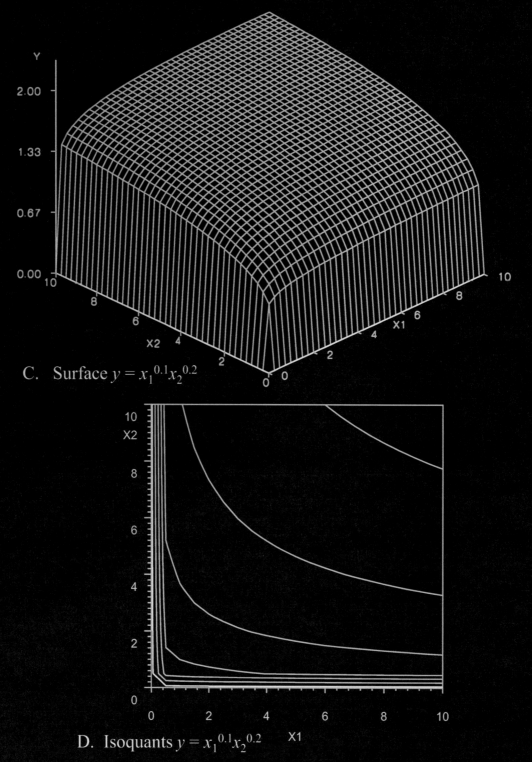

C. Surface $y = x_1^{0.1} x_2^{0.2}$

D. Isoquants $y = x_1^{0.1} x_2^{0.2}$

Figure 10.2 Surfaces and Isoquants for the Cobb-Douglas
Type Production Function

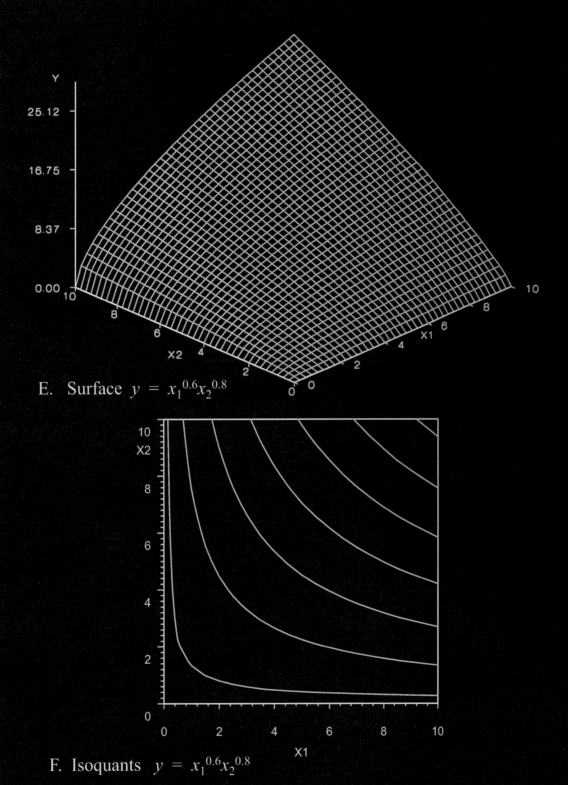

E. Surface $y = x_1^{0.6}x_2^{0.8}$

F. Isoquants $y = x_1^{0.6}x_2^{0.8}$

Figure 10.2 Surfaces and Isoquants for the Cobb-Douglas
Type Production Function

55

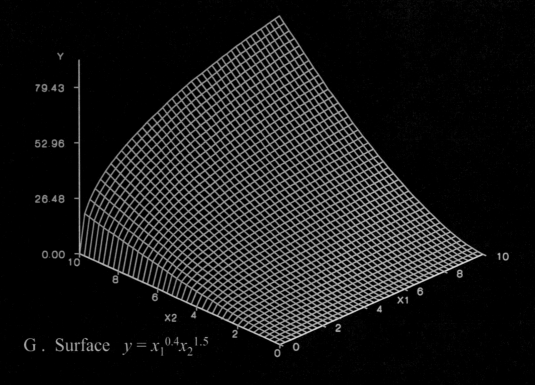

G . Surface $y = x_1^{0.4} x_2^{1.5}$

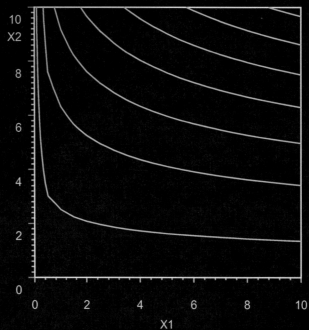

H. Isoquants $y = x_1^{0.4} x_2^{1.5}$

Figure 10.2 Surfaces and Isoquants for the Cobb-Douglas
Type Production Function

56

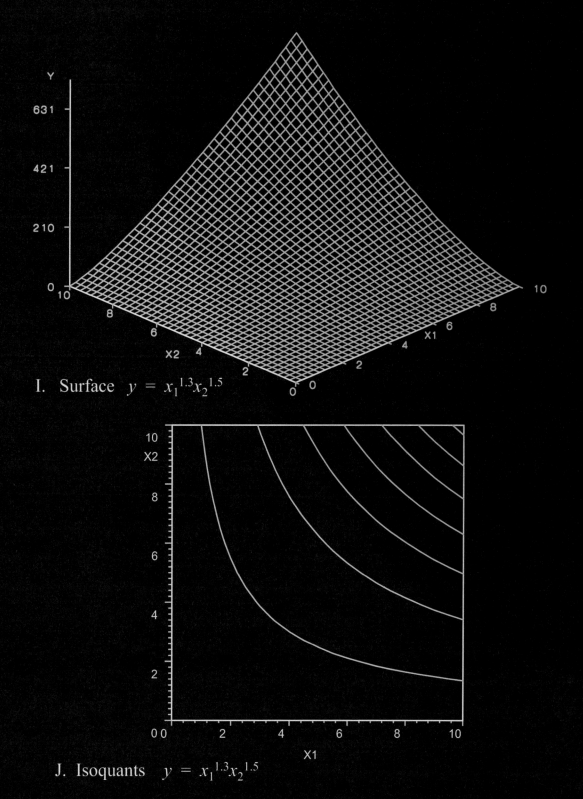

I. Surface $y = x_1^{1.3} x_2^{1.5}$

J. Isoquants $y = x_1^{1.3} x_2^{1.5}$

Figure 10.2 Surfaces and Isoquants for a Cobb-Douglas
Type Production Function

57

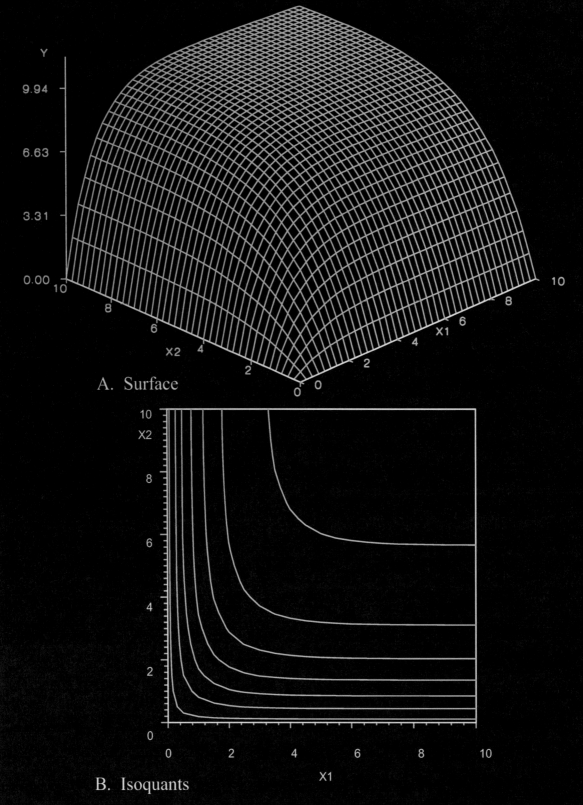

A. Surface

B. Isoquants

58   Figure 11.1 The Spillman Production Function

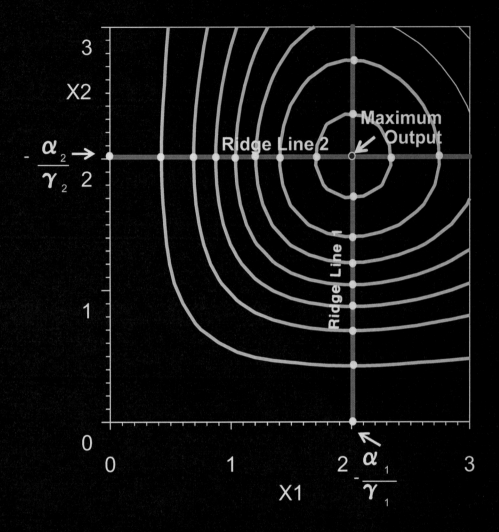

Figure 11.2 Isoquants and Ridge Lines for the Transcendental,
$\gamma_1 = \gamma_2$ -2; $\alpha_1 = \alpha_2 = 4$; $\gamma_3 = 0$

59

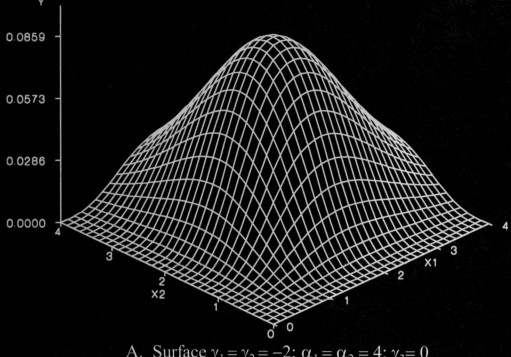

A. Surface $\gamma_1 = \gamma_2 = -2$; $\alpha_1 = \alpha_2 = 4$; $\gamma_3 = 0$

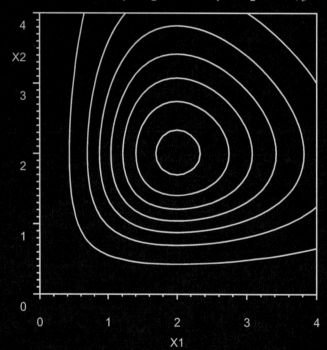

B. Isoquants $\gamma_1 = \gamma_2 = -2$; $\alpha_1 = \alpha_2 = 4$; $\gamma_3 = 0$

Figure 11.3 The Transcendental Production Function
Under Varying Parameter Assumptions

60

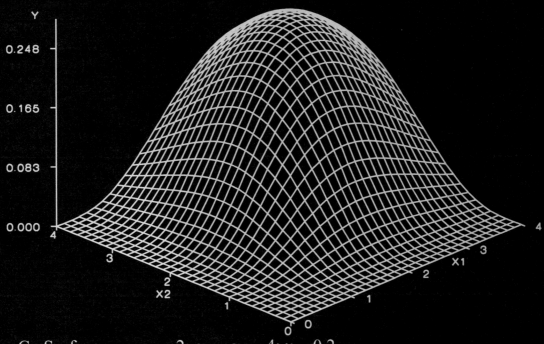

C. Surface $\gamma_1 = \gamma_2 = -2$; $\alpha_1 = \alpha_2 = 4$; $\gamma_3 = 0.2$

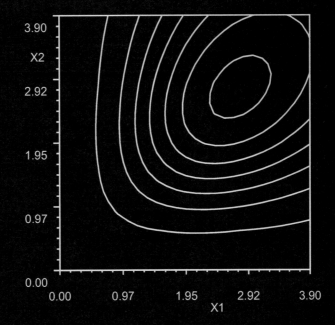

D. Isoquants $\gamma_1 = \gamma_2 = -2$; $\alpha_1 = \alpha_2 = 4$; $\gamma_3 = 0.2$

Figure 11.3 The Transcendental Production Function
Under Varying Parameter Assumptions   61

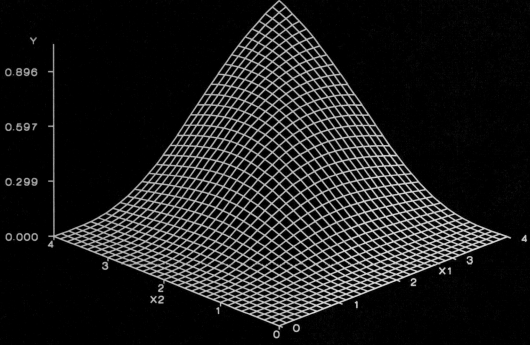

E . Surface $\gamma_1 = \gamma_2 = -2;\ \alpha_1 = \alpha_2 = 4;\ \gamma_3 = 0.3$

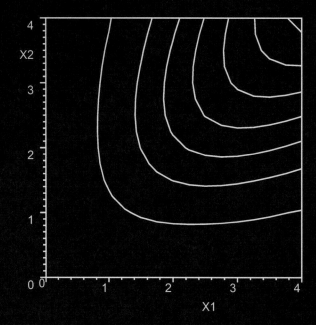

F.   Isoquants $\gamma_1 = \gamma_2 = -2;\ \alpha_1 = \alpha_2 = 4;\ \gamma_3 = 0.3$

Figure 11.3 The Transcendental Production Function
Under Varying Parameter Assumptions

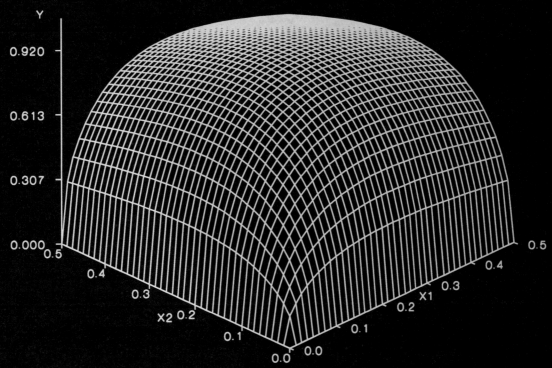

G. Surface $\gamma_1 = \gamma_2 = -2$; $\alpha_1 = \alpha_2 = 0.5$; $\gamma_3 = 0$

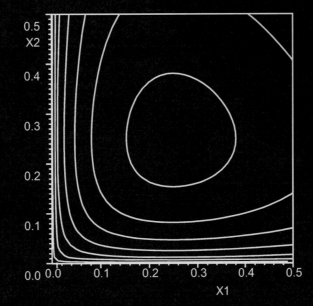

H. Isoquants $\gamma_1 = \gamma_2 = -2$; $\alpha_1 = \alpha_2 = 0.5$; $\gamma_3 = 0$

Figure 11.3 The Transcendental Production Function
Under Varying Parameter Assumptions

63

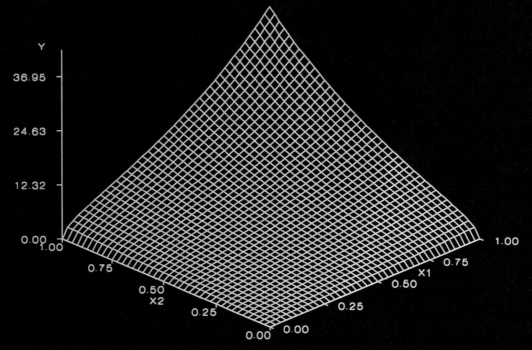

I. Surface $\gamma_1 = \gamma_2 = 1;\ \alpha_1 = \alpha_2 = 0.5;\ \gamma_3 = 0$

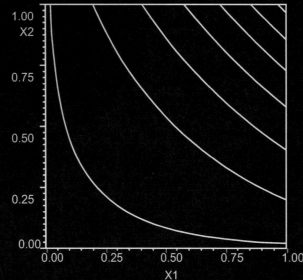

J. Isoquants $\gamma_1 = \gamma_2 = 1;\ \alpha_1 = \alpha_2 = 0.5;\ \gamma_3 = 0$

Figure 11.3 The Transcendental Production Function
Under Varying Parameter Assumptions

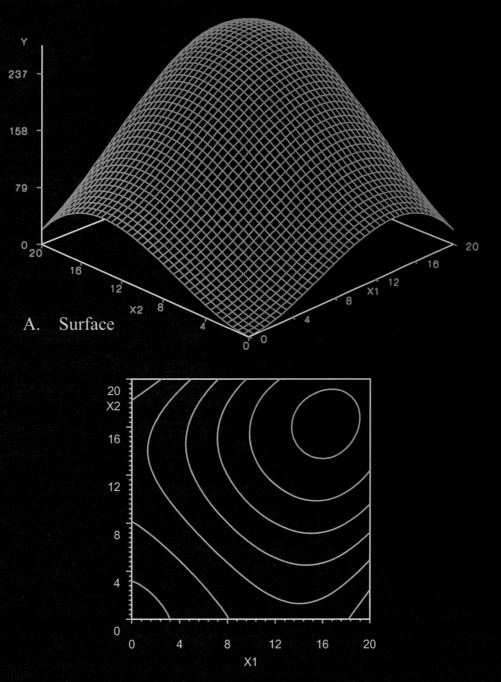

A. Surface

B. Isoquants

Figure 11.4 The Polynomial
$$y = x_1 + x_1^2 - 0.05\, x_1^3 + x_2 + x_2^2 - 0.05\, x_2^3 + 0.4\, x_1 x_2$$

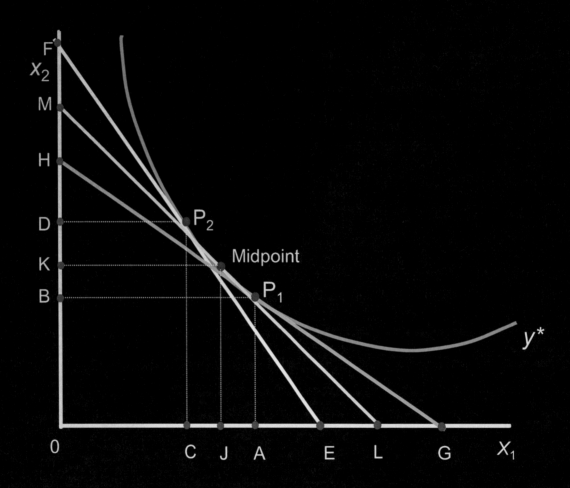

Figure 12.1 The Arc Elasticity of Substitution

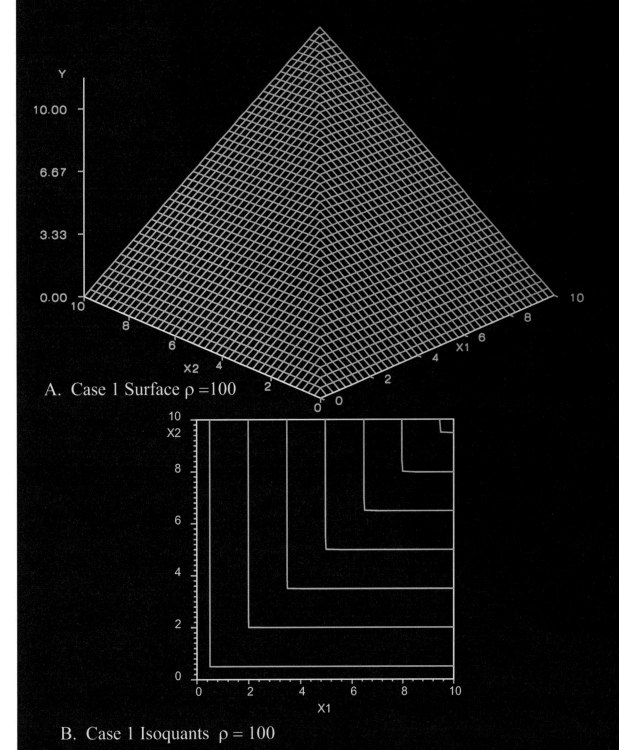

A. Case 1 Surface ρ =100

B. Case 1 Isoquants ρ = 100

Figure 12.2 Production Surfaces and Isoquants for the *CES* Production
Function under Varying Assumptions about ρ

67

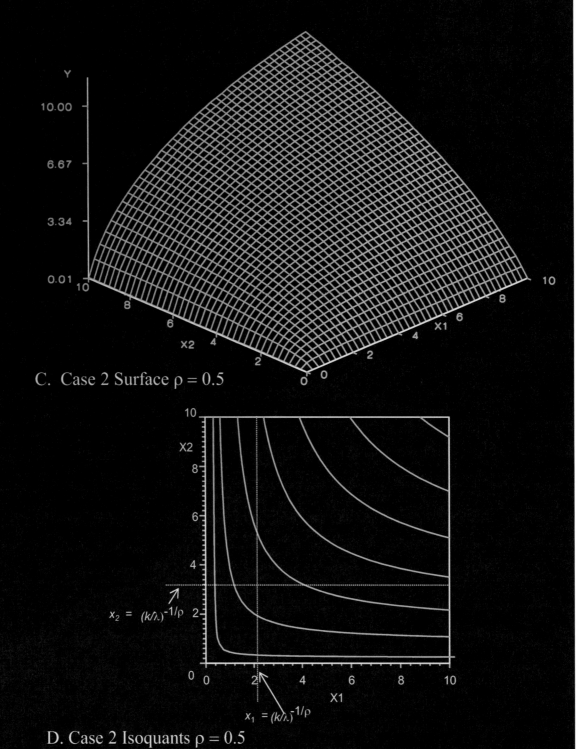

C. Case 2 Surface ρ = 0.5

D. Case 2 Isoquants ρ = 0.5

Figure 12.2 Production Surfaces and Isoquants for the *CES*
Production Function under Varying Assumptions about ρ

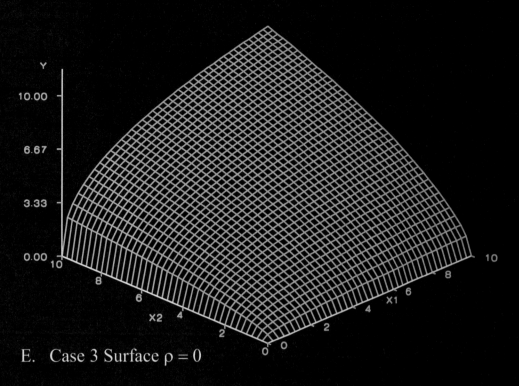

E. Case 3 Surface $\rho = 0$

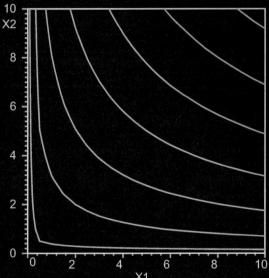

F. Case 3 Isoquants $\rho = 0$

Figure 12.2 Production Surfaces and Isoquants for the *CES* Production
Function under Varying Assumptions about ρ

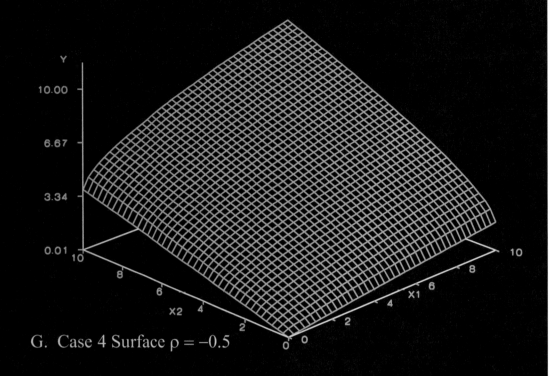

G. Case 4 Surface $\rho = -0.5$

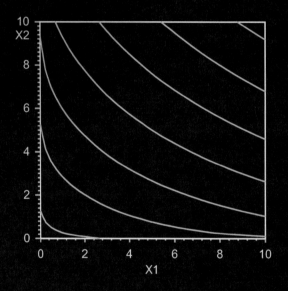

J Case 4 Isoquants $\rho = -0.5$

Figure 12.2 Production Surfaces and Isoquants for the *CES* Production
Function under Varying Assumptions about ρ

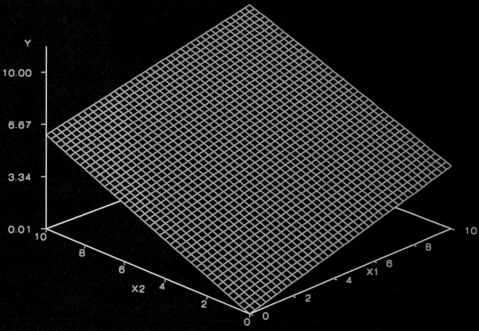

I . Case 5 Surface ρ approaches -1

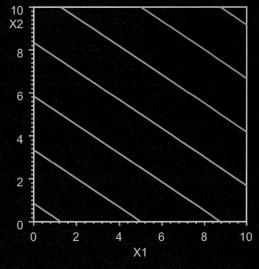

J. Case 5 Isoquants ρ approaches -1

Figure 12.2 Production Surfaces and Isoquants for the *CES* Production
Function under Varying Assumptions about ρ

71

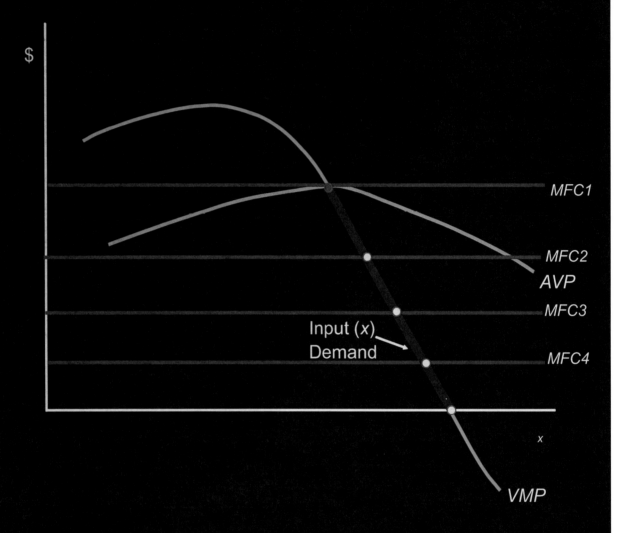

MFC1

MFC2
AVP

MFC3

Input (x)
Demand

MFC4

x

VMP

Figure 13.1 The Demand Function for Input x (No Other Inputs)

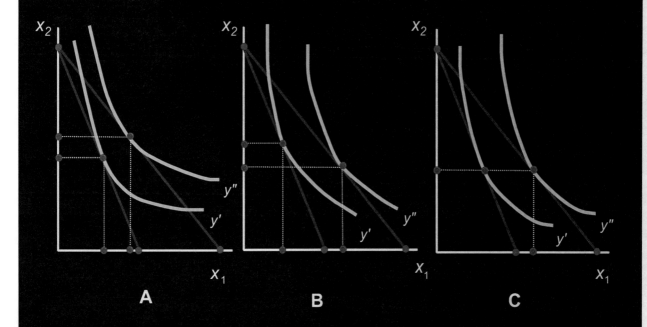

Figure 13.2 Possible Impacts of an Increase in the Price of x_1
on the use of x_2

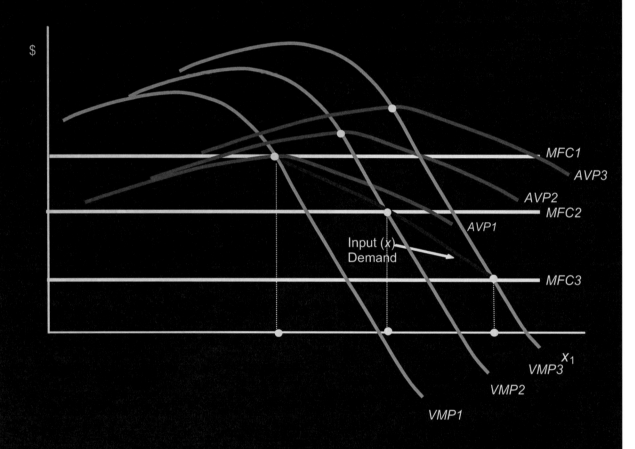

Figure 13.3 Demand for Input x_1 when a Decrease in the Price
of x_1 Increases the Use of x_2

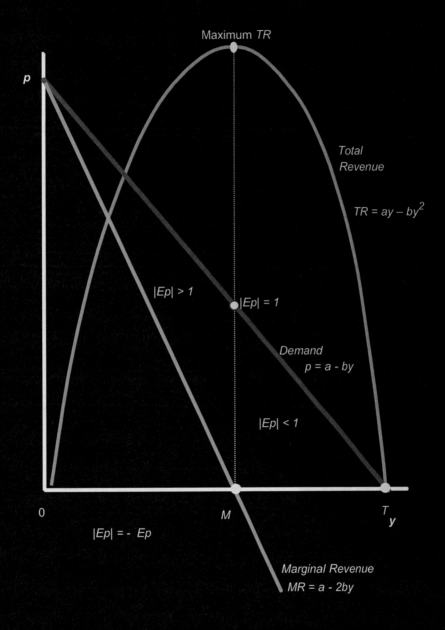

Figure 14.1 Total Revenue, Marginal Revenue,
and the Elasticity of Demand

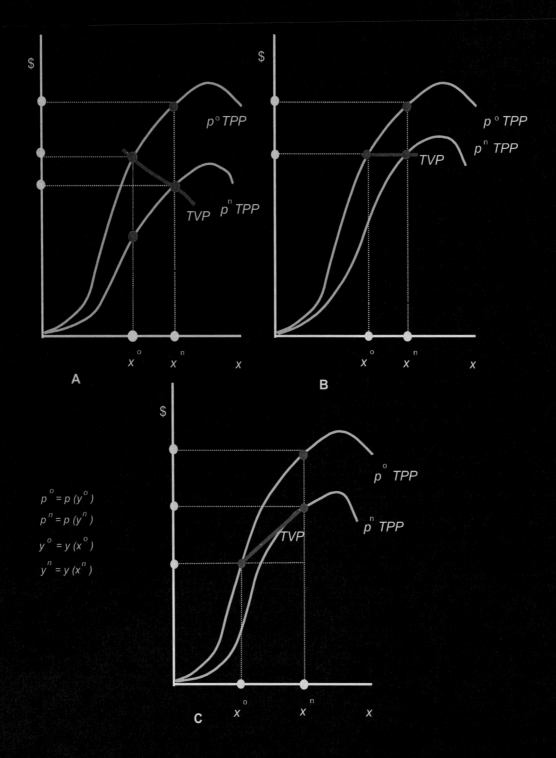

Figure 14.2 Possible *TVP* Functions Under Variable Product Prices

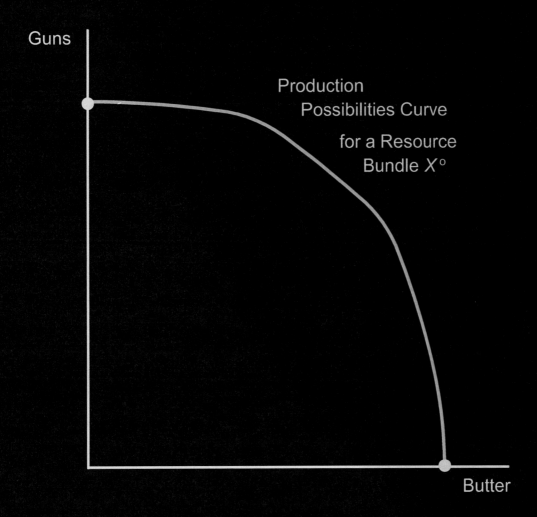

Figure 15.1 A Classic Production Possibilities Curve

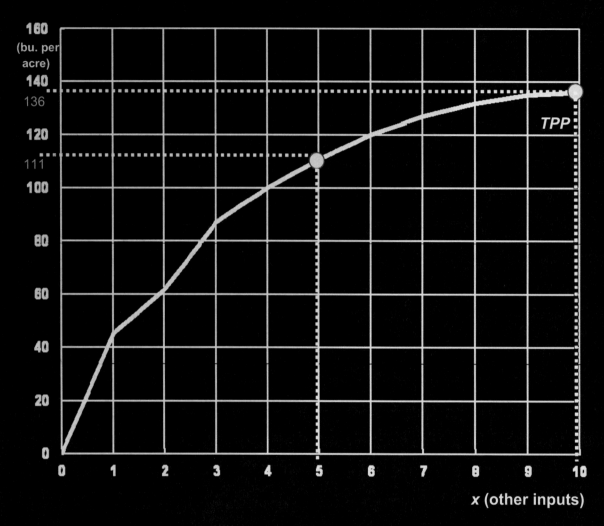

Corn

160 (bu. per acre) **140** 136 **120** 111 **100** **80** **60** **40** **20** **0**

TPP

0   1   2   3   4   5   6   7   8   9   10

x (other inputs)

Panel A

Figure 15.2 Deriving a Product Transformation
Function from Two Production Functions

Soybeans

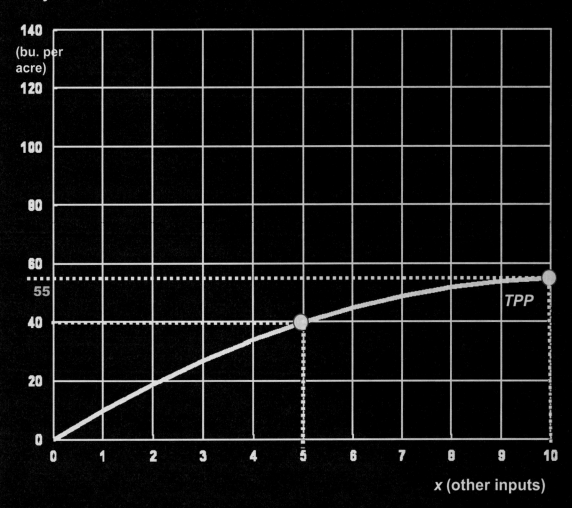

Panel B

Figure 15.2 Deriving a Product Transformation Function
from Two Production Functions

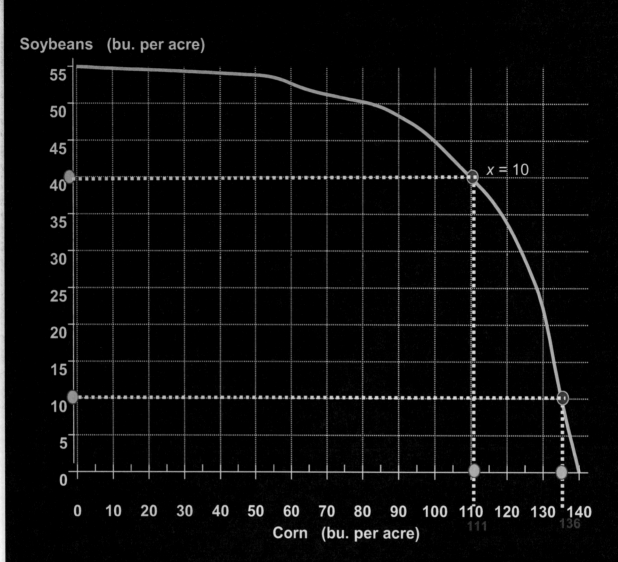

Panel C

Figure 15.2 Deriving a Product Transformation Function
                from Two Production Functions

80

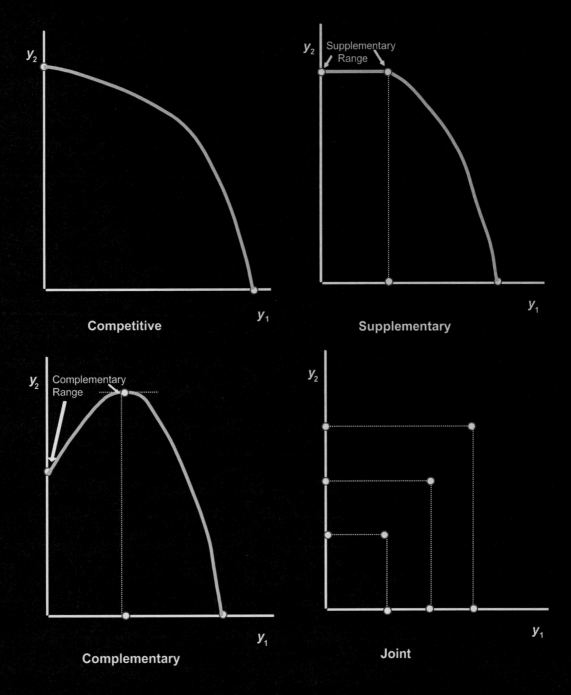

Figure 15.3   Competitive, Supplementary,
Complementary and Joint Products

81

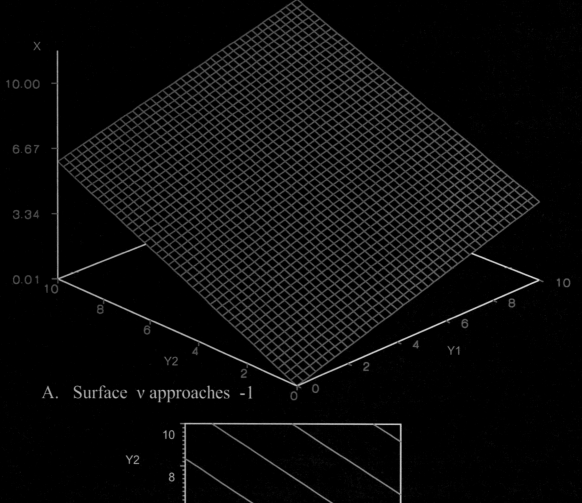

A. Surface ν approaches -1

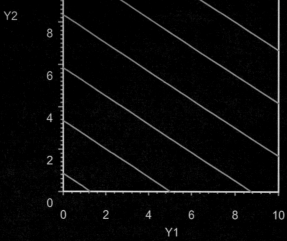

B. Isoproduct Contours ν approaches -1

Figure 15.4 Isoproduct Surfaces and Isoproduct Contours for a
CES Type of Function, ν < -1

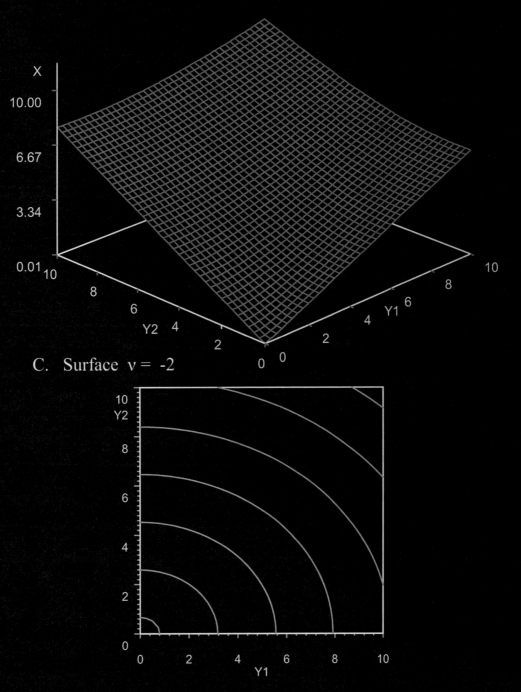

C. Surface ν = -2

D. Isoproduct Contours ν = -2

Figure 15.4 Isoproduct Surfaces and Isoproduct Contours
for a *CES* Type of Function, ν <-1

83

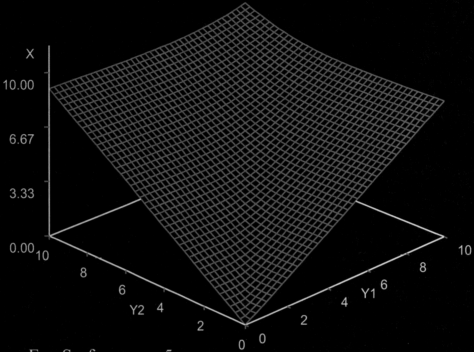

E. Surface $v = -5$

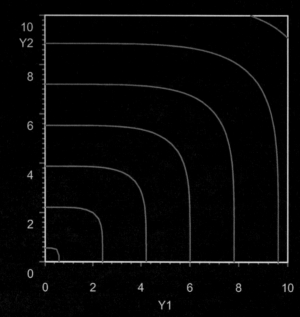

F. Isoproduct Contours $v = -5$

Figure 15.4 Isoproduct Surfaces and Isoproduct Contours
for a *CES* Type of Function, $v < -1$

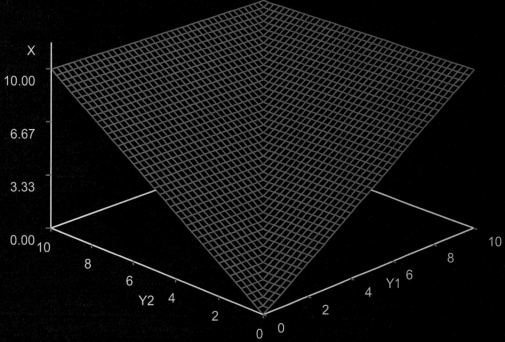

G. Surface ν = -200

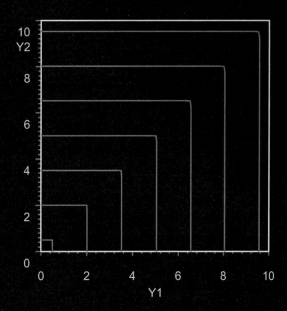

H. Isoproduct Contours ν = -200

Figure 15.4 Isoproduct Surfaces and Isoproduct Contours
for a *CES* Type of Function, ν < -1

85

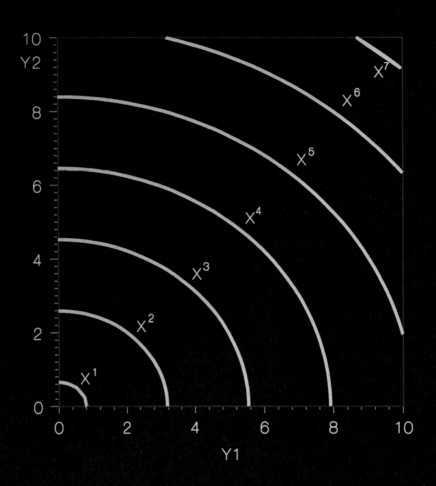

Figure 16.1 A Family of Product Transformation Functions

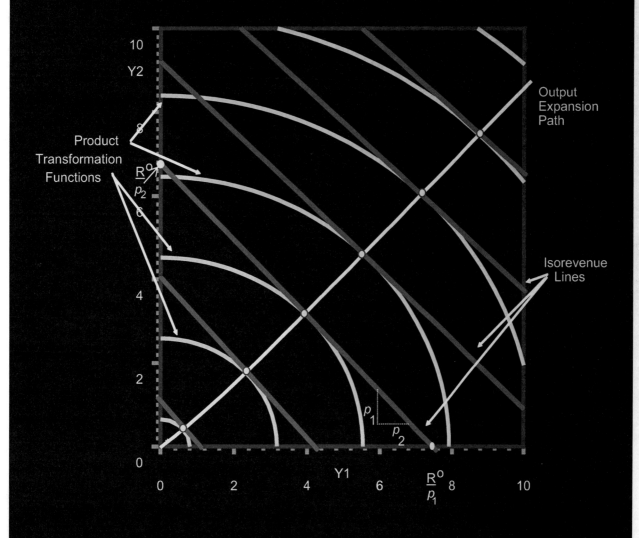

Figure 16.2 Product Transformation Functions, Isorevenue
Lines and the Output Expansion Path

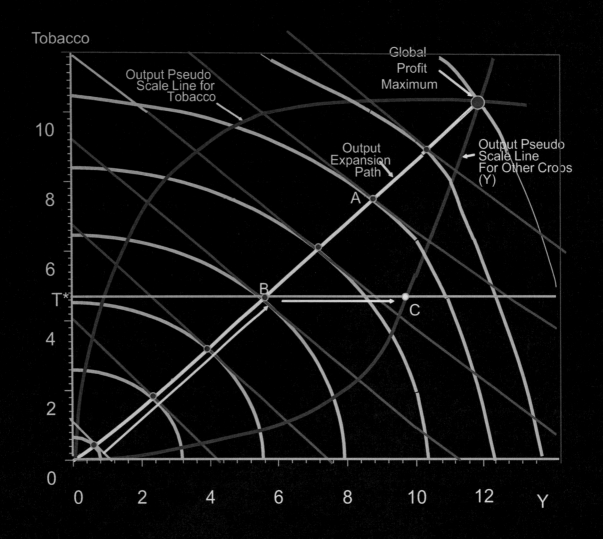

Figure 16.3 An Output Quota

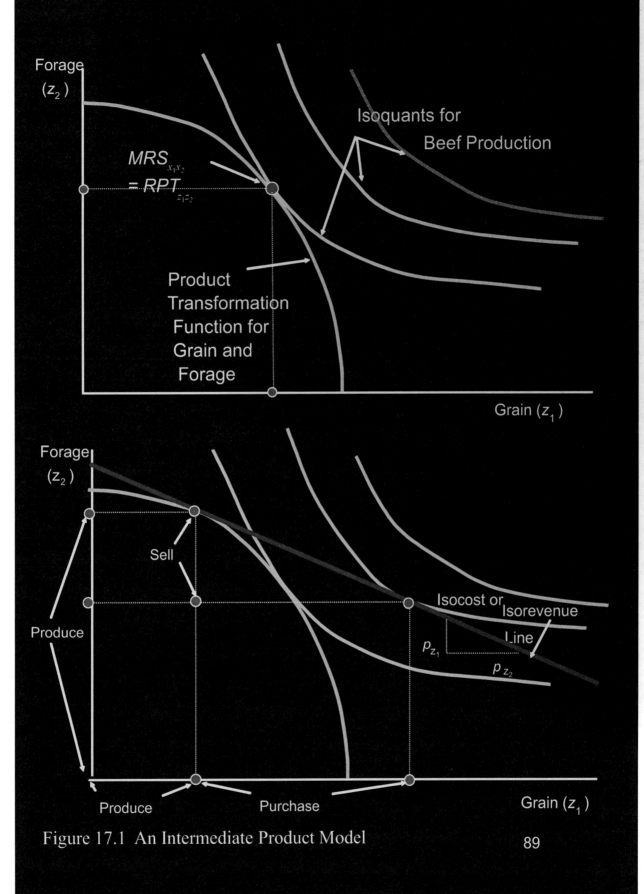

Figure 17.1 An Intermediate Product Model

89

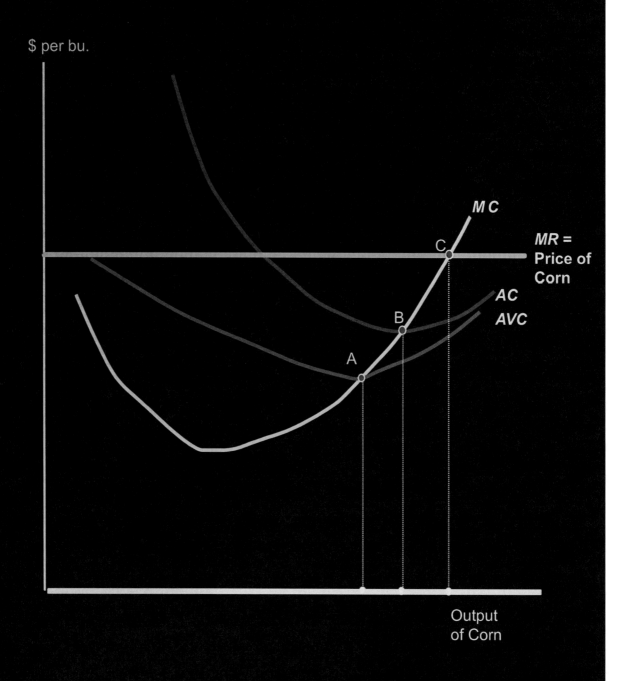

Figure 19.1 Output of Corn and Per Bushel Cost of Production

Probabilities
and Outcomes
are Known

Probabilities
And Outcomes
Are not known

Risky Events

Uncertain Events

Figure 20.1 A Risk and Uncertainty Continuum

91

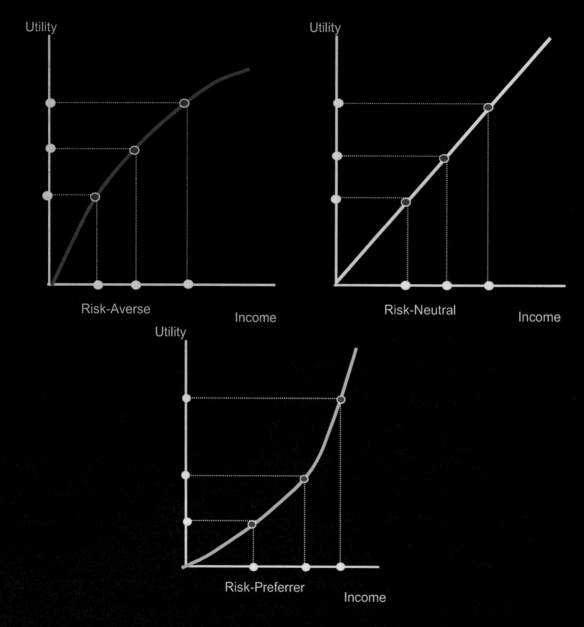

Figure 20.2 Three Possible Functions Linking Utility to Income

92

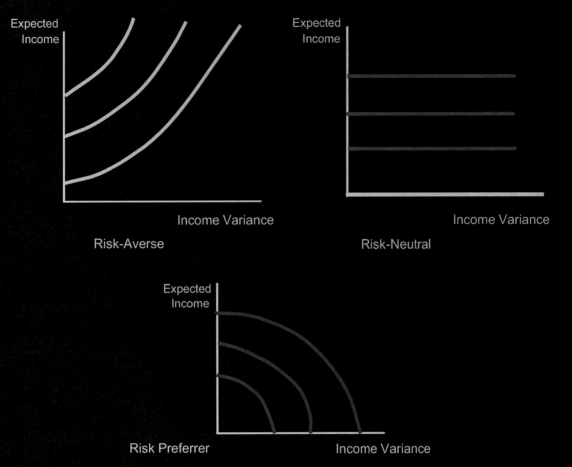

Figure 20.3 Indifference Curves Linking the Variance of
Expected Income with Expected Income

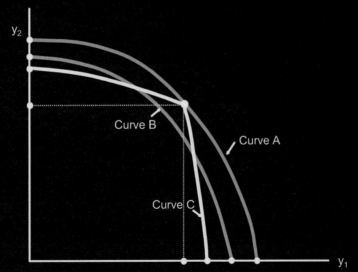

Figure 20.4 Long Run Planning: Specialized and Non-Specialized
Facilities

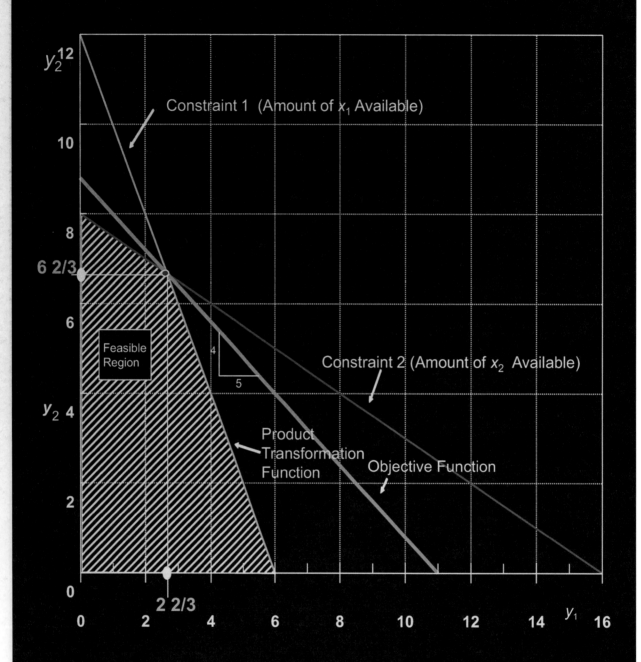

Figure 22.1 Linear Programming Solution in Product Space

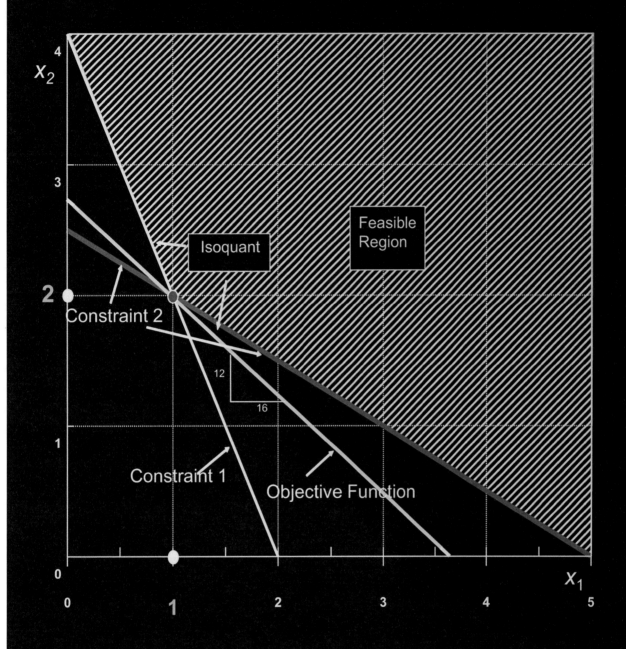

Figure 24.2 Linear Programming Solution in Factor Space

95

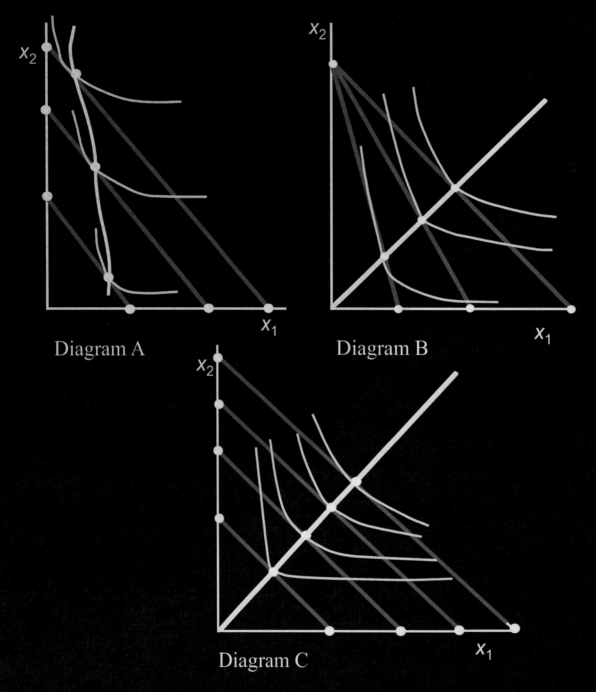

Figure 23.1 Some Possible Impacts of Technological Change

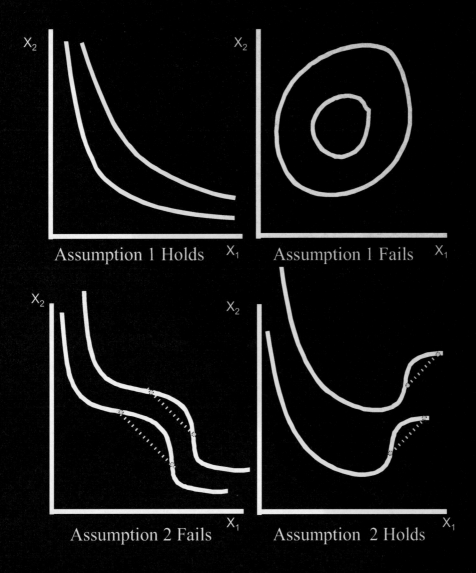

Figure 24.1 Assumptions (1) and (2) and the Isoquant Map

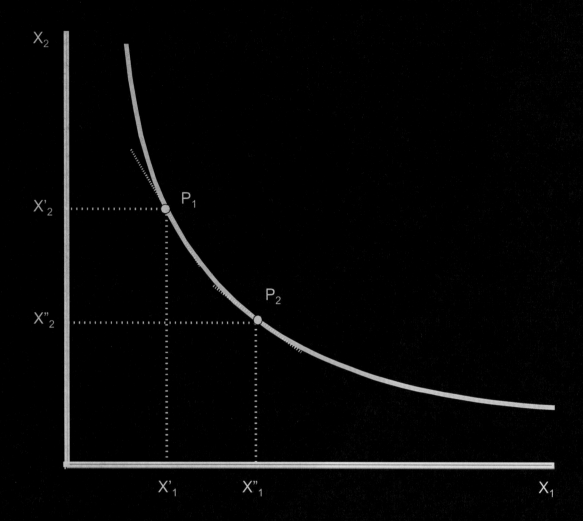

Figure 24.2 A Graphical Representation of the Elasticity of Substitution

Made in United States
North Haven, CT
07 July 2022